C000271471

Arthur Scholey's delighted interest in the work of Rumi (and also of Sa'di: see this book's companion volume, *The Discontented Dervishes*) began when he was asked to dramatise several of the stories for radio. The commission was an open sesame to a treasure store of the tales Rumi invented, collected and retold to weave into his mystical poetry.

This collection, here retold again, stems from Arthur Scholey's lifelong love of stories of all kinds – from folk tale, fable, saga, legend and parable, through to anecdote, joke and myths ancient and urban.

Collecting, creating and passing on stories, within today's fascinatingly burgeoning media, have led him to adapt others' and his own work in collections of his own and also for radio, tv, and stage performances. He also works with illustrators, and with composers on operas, dramatic cantatas and song collections. He lives in London.

By the same Author:

Stories, original, re-told, collected & illustrated

Twelve Tales for a Christmas Night

Sallinka and the Golden Bird

Baboushka

The Discontented Dervishes

The Scarab and the Fish

A Calendar of Christmas Wonder Tales

Plays & dramatisations

The Dickens Christmas Carol Show

Who'll be Brother Donkey?

Martin the Cobbler

The Hosanna Kids

Five Plays for Christmas

Operas & cantatas

The Song of Caedmon

Brendan Ahoy!

The Journey of the Christmas Creatures

Baboushka

Herod and the Rooster

Candletree, Wacky and his Fuddlejig

The Visitors

Singalive!

Tales from Rumi
retold by Arthur Scholey

The
Paragon
Parrot

And Other Inspirational
Tales of Wisdom

Watkins Publishing
London

This edition published in the UK in 2002 by
Watkins Publishing, 20 Bloomsbury Street,
London, WC1B 3QA

© Arthur Scholey 2002

Arthur Scholey has asserted his right under the
Copyright, Designs and Patents Act, 1988, to be identified
as author of this work.

All rights reserved.

No part of this book may be reproduced or utilized in any
form or by any means, electronic or mechanical, without
prior permission in writing from the Publishers.

Cover design by Echelon Design, Wimborne
Cover photograph © PhotoDisk
Designed and typeset by Echelon Design, Wimborne
Printed and bound in Great Britain by NFF Production

British Library Cataloguing in Publication data available

Library of Congress Cataloging in Publication data
available

ISBN 1 84293 046 X

From the bee, honey.
From the wasp, a sting.
Yet both drink from
the same flower!

Rumi

Contents

Contents

Contents

CONTENTS

CONTENTS

Contents

Foreword

'You are Layla! cries the ...
who has seen thy blood More ...
you have I can't understand it. It ...
beyond than any other woman.

For you are not Majnun, my Lord, I ...

The brief exchange evokes a sigh ... at time for we are all – or could be ... caught the I-and-the lover Imbibes ... by the thirteenth century mystery ... mystical and poetic work Mathnawi ... delights as much now with its ... early experience and birth as it did ... collected seven centuries ago.

The tales selected and retold here ... poetry of Rumi's work. The quatrains ... poetic couplets, quatrains and longer ... continued to delight and enchant, ... translated. The stories – down-to- ... gleaned from friends and folktales ... travels and travellers also embody ...

Foreword

'So you are Layla!' cries the Caliph. 'You're the one who has sent my friend Majnun out of his mind with love. I can't understand it. To me you are no more beautiful than any other woman.

'But you are not Majnun, my Lord,' Layla replies.

The brief exchange evokes a sigh, a nod, a smile, perhaps all three for we are all – or could be in our time – the caliph, the friend, the lover. Included among many tales by the thirteenth century mystic poet Rumi in his epic mystical and poetic work *Mathnawi*, it intrigues and delights as much now, with its insight and down-to-earth experience and truth, as it did when it was first collected seven centuries ago.

The tales, selected and retold here, give some introductory essence of Rumi's work. The epic's twenty thousand or so poetic couplets, quatrains and longer poems have continued to delight and enchant, and go on being translated. The stories – down-to-earth observations plucked from friends and folktales and real life, from travels and travellers, also embody Sufi wisdom, kindness, courtesy and candour, and contribute considerably to the work as a whole. As with parables they reverse and upset expectations, directing sudden shafts of insight and understanding. Some enter with banter and guffaw, others tend to wait in a corner of the soul, deftly putting in a word during a quiet moment.

Share then, the embarrassing truths a guest discovers by getting into the wrong bed, or the alarm of another guest who finds out – too late, too late! – where his poor monk hosts have obtained the wherewithal to feast him so lavishly. Watch how a noted rascal thief of a tailor is shamed and even at last forced actually to warn his naïve victim. As we pass the tattooist's shop, hear the agonised howls of the braggart who has ordered the lavish design ('Yowwww! What part of the lion is that?' 'Merely the first of the ears my dear sir.' 'Leave them out, leave them out, this lion will have to be deaf – well get on with the next bit – Ouch! Aaaghhh! Mercy ... !') Here are creatures both magical and foolish, a courteous camel, an ambitious ant, a hare exploiting the pride of a lion, a parrot who escapes his cage by decoding a secret message. Meet rulers wise and foolish, sort out good servants from bad, rejoice with one who finds treasure in the last place he expects it. Savour aphorism, riddle, puzzle – and a meeting which surprises even the Angel of Death.

While the poetry shares and contemplates the apparent simplicity of the tales, it is interesting to note, from another of Rumi's works, *The Discourses*, that early in life he tended to downplay his verses. I do it to occupy and interest my friends and guests, that's all, he said. But really I think little of it, and do have no more regard for it than the man who plunges his hands into the washing of the offal delicacies ready for the dinner table.

But this was to change when, towards the end of his thirties, Rumi met in his home streets of Iconium (now Konya in Turkey) a wandering dervish mystic, Shams ad-dīn. Rumi had all his life, of course, come under the influence of many mystics; his father was a noted mystic theologian and, when forced to leave his native land (in what is now Afghanistan) because of the Mongol invasion threat, the young Rumi was, according to legend, blessed by a noted author of mystical epics during the journey to Rum (now Anatolia in Turkey and hence his eventual name). Here he met and was influenced by many more mystics and eventually at the age of twenty-four, when his father died, took over and became esteemed as teacher and preacher.

The wandering mystic Shams, though, was different. Rumi became deeply attached to him and they lived together for two years, to the growing and eventually scandalised dismay of his neglected wife and sons, friends, colleagues and disciples. None of these could appreciate the fascination of the wild dervish (but then, *they* weren't Rumi!). He was going through a deep emotional and spiritual relationship, a revelation of divine love and beauty – which broke off disastrously when his family forced Shams out of Iconium and he was allegedly murdered.

The distraught Rumi now poured into poetry – and from his heart – his loss, yearning and love, so identifying and uniting himself with Shams that he put the dervish's name instead of his own to some of his poetry, a chronicle of the development of a relationship reaching ecstatic heights – interweaving within it the down-to-earth candour of the tales. Also influencing it were rhythm, drumming, dancing and music (the soulful flute, for example, which eventually became so much a feature of the Mevlevi order of Whirling Dervishes founded in Rumi's name). The spiritual couplets, quatrains and verses poured out of Rumi while he walked, talked, preached and taught, bathed and danced; faithful disciples recorded them for inclusion in the work to come.

The tales retold here, then, are offered as good stories in themselves, and as tasters for those who might be tempted to go on in to the banquet of Rumi's work.

Don't in either case, though, devour them all at once! Dip and dive ...

The Paragon Parrot

...and other tales about
learning from experience

The Paragon Parrot

*T*HERE WAS once a greengrocer who had a most talkative and clever parrot. Every day it sat with him on a bench in the shop, chatting and even selling the goods to the customers. Increasingly, on the many occasions when the greengrocer had to slip away, he quite happily left the parrot in charge.

However, on one of the days when the greengrocer was out, the parrot, in flying from the bench to perch, accidentally knocked over a bottle of rose oil. The greengrocer did not immediately notice this when he returned. He sat down on the bench and only then, as the oil gradually seeped into his clothes, did he realise what had happened, and who the culprit must be. Angrily he jumped up and fetched the parrot such a clout that all the feathers fell off its head.

As soon as he had done it, the greengrocer was sorry. But he was even more sorry to discover that his now bald parrot seemed also to have lost the gift of speech. Day after day passed; not a word came from the parrot.

The greengrocer tore his beard, and begged the parrot's forgiveness.

'I wish my hand had dropped off,' he cried. 'How could I have done such a thing?' But the parrot remained silent. The greengrocer went out into the street, with gifts for every holy man and beggar he met, in the hope that his generosity might bring speech back to the parrot.

But there was no response.

After three days of this the greengrocer sank down on his bench in utter despair. He had tried everything he could think of, but still the parrot did not speak.

At that moment an old holy man passed by the shop; he was poor, dressed in a coarse robe – and with not a hair on his head.

Suddenly the parrot stirred, flapped its wings, opened its beak, and spoke:

'Hey there, Baldie,' it called out. 'Have you been spilling the oil as well?'

The Lion's Share

*C*OME IN, come in!' roared the lion to the wolf and the fox who stood timidly outside his cave. 'I can see you have something on your mind. What is it? Don't be afraid.'

'We have a suggestion to put to you, O King,' said the wolf. 'It's only a suggestion, mind.'

'I'll hear it,' said the lion graciously. The wolf looked at the fox.

'It's like this,' said the fox. 'We were wondering if you could possibly agree to letting us join you when you go out hunting, that we - ahem! - work together as a team.'

'I'm sure we'd catch more animals that way,' the wolf added nervously. They waited.

The lion glared at them, frowned, thought a bit, then nodded his head, and agreed. Immediately they set off for the mountain regions in search of their prey.

Now, you might have thought that the lion, a magnificent beast in ferocious prime, would secretly be rather ashamed to be seen in league with such insignificant creatures, and you would have been right. He had no need of their help to catch his meat. However, he had decided to go along with them as a special concession.

'I will honour these two with my presence', he said to himself, 'I hope, for their sakes, that they appreciate it, that's all!'

Well, they had a good hunt and at the end of an hour they gathered round the spoil. The lion looked at the fox and the wolf as they greedily eyed the carcasses of a wild ox, a goat, and a hare.

'I do believe', he said to himself, 'that these two think they deserve an equal share of all this. Well, well, we'll see about that!'

He smiled at the fox and the wolf.

'Now, come along, old wolf', he said, 'let us have your ideas as to how we should divide all this up, eh? What are your views?'

'Well, King', said the wolf, 'it's fairly obvious that you must have the ox. He is big, and you are the biggest among us, certainly. The goat shall be mine, as it is of middle size, like me. As for the hare, that must go to the fox, of course.'

The lion roared in anger. 'What cheek,' he fumed, 'to presume even to try to divide the spoil in the glory of my presence. In the presence of the King, do you dare to say: You shall have that, I will have this? Where is the respect, the awe due to a royal beast?'

With that, the furious lion leaped upon the wolf and tore him to bits.

Then the lion turned to the fox. 'Now, you have a go,' he growled.

The fox trembled and bowed low to the earth. 'O excellent King,' he whispered at last, 'this fat ox shall be your royal breakfast. This tasty goat must be reserved for your victorious majesty at mid-day. And at the evening, O gracious and bountiful monarch, the juicy hare shall be your supper.'

'Wise and clever fox!' cried the lion. YOU have decided rightly, and as a reward you shall have all three animals for yourself. But now, tell me from whom you have learned such wisdom.'

7

'From the wolf, O king, from the wolf!' cried the fox. But he muttered to himself: 'What a blessing the lion asked *him* first!'

Checkmate!

*D*ALQAK, AN EXPERT chess player, was
summoned to play a game with the Prince –
and quickly beat him.

'Checkmate!' he cried triumphantly.

Up rose the Prince in fury. He seized the heavy,
gold chessmen one by one, and threw them
violently at Dalqak's head. All poor Dalqak could
do was cower at his feet, pleading:

'Mercy! Mercy!'

So, imagine Dalqak's feelings when a further
summons came from the Prince to play another
game! In fear and trembling, he sat down to play.
After the game had progressed for a little, he
suddenly jumped up, ran into a corner of the room
and dived under a pile of rugs.

'Come out from under there!' the Prince bellowed.
'What is the meaning of this?'

Dalqak peeped timidly from under the rugs and whispered fearfully:

'Checkmate?'

How the Donkey Learned to be Content

*T*HE WATER-CARRIER'S donkey - what a miserable creature he was! Bent almost double by his load, with a hundred sores on his back, all he looked forward to was death.

Barley? This poor creature never saw any. Straw was all he got - and not enough of that. However, he got more than he wanted of his master's goading and heavy blows.

One day the Master of the Royal Stable caught sight of him - the donkey's master was known to him - and took pity on the beast.

'How come your donkey is in such a state? He's bent double, my friend.'

'How can he help being in that state,' replied the owner, 'seeing my own wretched poverty?'

'He certainly needs a rest,' said the Master of the Royal Stable. 'Tell you what: hand him over to me for a few days. I'll quarter him in the King's stable. He'll soon be fit and strong again.'

The donkey's owner was delighted and readily agreed. Soon the astonished donkey found himself in a luxurious stable. On either side of him were magnificent Arabian horses, well fed, glossy and handsome.

His stall was swept every day and sprinkled with fresh water; new clean straw was put down; delicious barley appeared, always at the expected time.

As he looked at his gleaming stable mates, preening themselves as they were being combed and rubbed down, the donkey cried: 'Lord in glory, am I not also one of your creatures? O, it's true I'm only a donkey, but is that any reason why I should have such a wretched existence, sleepless through the night because of my aching back and empty belly? How often I've longed for death, yet look at these rich and happy creatures! Why was I singled out for pain and misery?'

Suddenly there was a fanfare of trumpets, the rat-a-tat of drums and cries of 'To war! To war!' The stable filled with warriors, the horses were saddled and ridden off amid great excitement.

Later that day some of them returned. They staggered in, collapsed and lay gasping on their backs, whimpering with the pain of the arrows that suck into them. Vets stood by with scalpels and the cry of the horses was pitiful as the vets struggled to get out the cruel barbs.

It was in the midst of this terrible scene that the donkey whispered: 'Lord? Are you there? Forget my complaints, I beg you. I'm content with my lot. I'll do without the rich life if these wounds are the price of it.'

First on the Prayer List

'*L*ORD, BLESS the criminals of this world,' prayed the preacher. 'Let thy mercy be on all evil-doers, upon those who corrupt others and those who break the law with insolence. Those who take advantage of goodness in others, let them know Thy mercy, too.'

'What nonsense is this?' muttered the congregation. 'Whoever heard of prayers for the wicked? Why does he pray for *them* even before the innocent and good?'

The preacher overheard and called down:

'The reason is because I have always benefited from coming into contact with these folk. That's why I pray for them. They do so much evil, injustice and oppression that they drive me to the opposite extreme, to do good! Whenever I encounter them in the world, their blows and beatings immediately drive me back to the holy sanctuaries. It is their wolves who force me to walk in the true way. So, as they are the main means of my salvation, I feel it my duty to pray for them first whenever I can.'

Who's There?

A MAN knocked at the door of a friend.

'Who's there?' the friend called.

'It is I', the man replied.

'Go away, then, there is no room for another here.'

The poor man spent a year in travel and then returned to his friend's door. Fearfully, he knocked.

'Who's there?'

'It is you, dear friend.'

He was made welcome.

The Caliph's Reward

. . . and other stories of gifts and generosity

The Caliph's Reward

IT WAS IN the middle of the night that a poor Bedouin woman cried out to her husband.

How is it that we alone suffer misery and poverty? Everyone else in the world lives in happiness and contentment...

At first her husband pretended not to listen, and went on.

How can I sleep? I'm hungry! Wallace we break our only salt is that of bitter anguish and my... our only unfailing supply of water is that which flows from our eyes. We have no clothes except the burning sky by day and the...

The husband tried to snore.

"I know you're not really asleep..."

The Caliph's Reward

*I*T WAS IN the middle of the night that a poor Bedouin woman cried out to her husband:

'How is it that we alone suffer hardships and poverty? Everyone else in the world lives in happiness and contentment, but look at us!'

At first her husband pretended not to hear, as she went on.

'How can I sleep? I'm hungry! We have no bread; our only salt is that of bitter anguish and envy; our only unfailing supply of water is that which flows from our eyes. We have no clothes except the burning sun by day and the moon by night.'

The husband tried to snore.

'I know you're not really asleep,' she cried. 'Even the worst of beggars feels ashamed at our poverty. Not only our relatives, but strangers as well avoid us like the plague.'

She gave him a nudge.

'Why don't you do something? Well? O, what's the use?'

Her husband sighed, stirred, and put his arm round his wife. 'Peace, wife,' he murmured. 'We are approaching the end of our lives. We should be reaching tranquility and contentment, not striving for wealth and goods.'

'Here we go again,' his wife fumed to herself. 'Any minute now it will be the birds and the beasts. You see!'

'Think how the birds and beasts live from day to day without worrying,' said her husband. 'Listen to that nightingale, singing thanks to God for its daily bread.'

'I can't bear it!' she screamed, jumping out of bed. The Bedouin called out to her:

'All your distress comes from desire, my dear. Remember, when you were young, how contented you were? Now you have become a mere seeker after gold; but when you were young you were gold itself! You were a rich vine, then, and your fruit should become sweeter as year follows year. So do stop your complaining. You know, we two should be as comfortable together as a pair of old shoes – but if one of the shoes starts to nip then not just one but the pair is useless.

In this way the Bedouin attempted to pacify his wife as the dawn broke. But she would have nothing of it.

'Hypocrite!' she cried, 'I won't listen to your speeches any longer. All this is your idea of religion. This talk of contentment – it's all show, all deceit! You can't beguile me with pious talk.'

'You're a devil, not the woman I married', cried the man angrily. 'I take pride in my poverty and have spent all my life in the desert. You have shared this, so why do you now beat me with all these complaints? Do you not understand spiritual things any more? What's the matter with you? There is richness in my soul, but how can I share it with you if you are not able to listen?'

At this the wife suddenly burst into tears.

'Forgive me', she sobbed. 'I'm not worthy to be your wife. You're a good man. I don't mind poverty, really, and it's you I'm thinking about when I complain.'

Her tears melted him.

'I'm sorry I was angry' he said. 'O light of my life, forgive me. Come, command me. I'll do what you think, without debating right and wrong, good and evil. I love you, and love will make me blind to everything but your interest.'

'It's a trick!' said the wife.

'No, no', the Bedouin assured her. 'I swear to you, I'll do whatever you command.'

'Well', she said, 'we've got to do something or we'll surely starve to death. Why don't you go to the Caliph and ask him to help us? Baghdad, where he lives, is alive with prosperity and gladness. He is like a sun shining over the world, so why shouldn't we benefit a little from his glory? It's worth trying, don't you think?'

The husband groaned.

'I can't just go into his presence without a reason', he said. 'It's no good trying to appear before a Caliph, simply saying: "I'm poor". I'll never get past the guards at the door.'

'Then take him a gift!' cried the wife. 'What is the

22

most precious thing we have, the most valuable
thing that any desert dweller possesses? Water, of
course. Take this jug of the last of our rain water.
Say to him: "You, O King, may have the greatest
treasure of gold and jewels in the world, yet this
that I offer you is the rarest and most precious
possession we Bedouins have."'

'You're right!' the husband agreed. 'He may be the
king of the world, but he can't possibly have water
as valuable as this. I'll do it.'

So the wife sealed her best green jug, sewed it up in
felt, and off went her husband while she prayed:

'O keep this precious water safe from robbers. Each
drop is as precious as a pearl. Watch over my
husband, O Lord, so that it arrives safely at its
destination.'

The Bedouin did arrive safely at the Caliph's court
and was immediately overwhelmed at what he saw.
Not a moment passed without some beggar getting
a gift. Petitioners cried with joy at having wishes
granted; gifts and robes of honour were given freely.
All were made welcome, and the generosity of the
Caliph could not be shown more clearly.

The Caliph's officers now approached the Bedouin
and welcomed him graciously. They could see his
tattered cloak and they guessed therefore what he
wanted. Nevertheless, they greeted him kindly:

'Are you tired after your long journey?' they asked.
'Welcome, O Arabian chieftain.'

'Arabian chieftain!' the man exclaimed. 'Hardly that,
I'm afraid, but thank you for the compliment! No,
I'm a poor stranger from the desert, that's all, and
I'm hoping that the Caliph will be generous to me.
If I'm a chieftain it is because of the spirit of this
place. It has ennobled me. So now, I beg you, bear
this before the Caliph. It's sweet rain-water in our
best green jug!'

The officials could not help smiling. Nevertheless
they looked upon the gift as if it were as precious as
life itself and in this they reflected the grace and
courtesy of the Caliph for it was his grace that
shone throughout the whole palace.

The officials led him to the chief minister who
bowed and escorted him through the Great Hall
and the Court of Golden Pillars into the throne
room itself. Trembling, the Bedouin was drawn to
the steps leading up to the throne. He dared not

look up, so he did not see the Caliph smile, nor see him descend until the Caliph touched his shoulder.

'Your Majesty', the Bedouin stammered but could say no more. All he could do was hold out his gift.

'Treasure indeed!' the Caliph said. 'Water from the desert, if I am not mistaken?' He accepted the cup and drank the contents to the last drop. 'Chief minister', he called, 'See, I have emptied this good man's cup. So now we shall fill it again, with gold. Bring him fresh robes and see that he has a place at my table for dinner. And tomorrow, when he is rested, let him return by way of my gardens.'

So it was that next morning, carrying his gold and still weeping with joy, the Bedouin strolled through the gardens. And then, beyond the trees, he caught sight of something he had never seen before - the sparkling, pure, clear waters of the great river Tigris.

He fell on his knees in wonder.

'O great Caliph', he cried. 'To think that you so graciously accepted my poor gift when you have all this! Truly, truly, you have rewarded my abject wealth - with your own . . .'

The Mouse and the Camel

A CHEEKY mouse was walking through the market place when he came across a dangling rope. He caught hold of it in his little paws and pulled it. The rope gave, so he pulled a bit harder. Still the rope gave so he walked on a bit with the rope over his shoulder.

Only then did he look up. At the other end of the rope was a camel!

However, the camel seemed content to be led, so, now with a haughty swagger the mouse gave a jerk of the rope and continued on his way, with the camel following.

'Hey, look at me!' he called out to all his friends and relatives. 'See, I told you I was a hero.'

'Hoho!' thought the camel, 'Hero, eh? Just you wait, little fellow.'

On they went, until they came to the bank of a great river. The waters rushed by in a great torrent.

Even a wolf or a lion would have trembled at the thought of crossing it.

The mouse was rigid with fear. The camel coughed discreetly.

'What's the matter, O my master?' he asked. 'Why have we stopped?'

'The river!' shivered the mouse. 'I shall be drowned.'

'Nonsense,' said the camel. 'I'll show you.' He stepped forward into the waters. 'Look, it's only up to my knee. What's the matter with you?'

'There's a difference between your knee and mine!' cried the mouse.

'About the same difference as there is between a mouse and a camel, my bold fellow?'

'I'm sorry!' said the mouse.

The camel laughed. 'Come on! Climb up, and sit on my hump. That's it. Now, hang on.'

And across they went together.

The Gift of Silence

A CERTAIN LORD was renowned for his generosity to beggars. Each morning, a different set received help from him: on one day all the sick were helped, on another widows, or holy men, students, outcasts, debtors, and so on. In this way he made sure that his generosity went to as many classes of the needy as possible.

He had one rule only with regard to his giving: this was that no-one should actually beg for gold, or even make a sound. Anyone who did so was ignored completely and went away empty-handed.

His motto was 'Be silent and you will be saved.'

In all his long life of generosity, it is said that only two men broke the rule of silence and yet received his help.

The first was an old man who cried out: 'Help me, Lord, for I am starving.' The people were astonished at him and the Lord stopped and said: 'Shameless old man!'

'Not as shameless as you, sir', the old man replied. 'You have wealth enough to enjoy this world to the full, but, not content with that, you are hoping, with all this so-called generosity, to enjoy the next world as well!'

This made the Lord laugh so much that he gave the old man some money.

The second man was a poor law student who, on the day when it was the turn of law-students to receive help, began to whine and beg. He got nothing.

On the following day it was the turn of the sick, so the student tied splints to his leg and stood in the queue with his head drooping. But the Lord recognised him and he got nothing.

On the next day the student drew a cloak over his head and sat among the widows. But the Lord recognised him even in this disguise - and so with every trick the student tried.

At last the student went to an undertaker and said: 'Wrap me up in a shroud and lay me out on the road where the Lord passes. It may be that he will recognise me and, thinking I am dead, will at last be moved to give the cost of the shroud. If he does, I'll give you half of it.'

The undertaker did what he asked and, later that day, the Lord passed by – and dropped some gold on the shroud. Fearful that the undertaker might steal the lot the student pushed his hand out to take the money. His movement disturbed the shroud and his trick was revealed.

'Well, Lord,' he cried, 'at last I have a gift from you who persistently refused to help me.'

'So I see,' commented the Lord drily, 'however, you had to die to get it!'

The Lion
and The Hare

*...three tales of difficulties
overcome by cleverness*

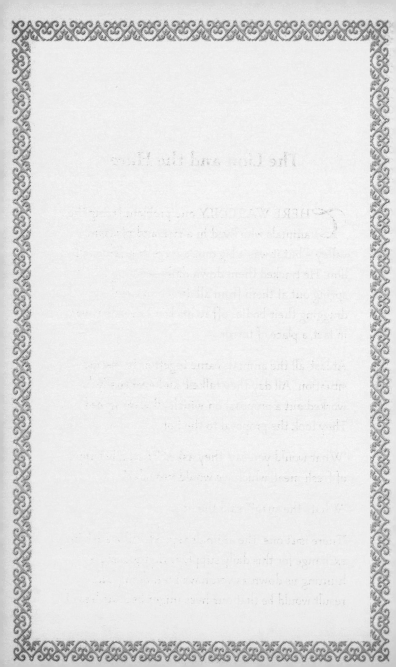

The Lion and the Hare

THERE WAS ONLY one problem facing the animals who lived in a rich and pleasant valley – but it was a big one: a huge and ferocious lion. He tracked them down daily, seeming to spring out at them from all directions, and dragging their bodies off to his lair. The valley was, in fact, a place of terror.

At last, all the animals came together to discuss the situation. All day they talked, and eventually worked out a proposal on which all were agreed. They took the proposal to the lion.

'What would you say', they asked 'to a daily supply of fresh meat, which we would provide?'

'What's the snag?' said the lion.

'There isn't one', the animals replied. 'All we ask in exchange for this daily supply is that you stop hunting us down as you have been doing. The result would be that our lives might become less of a nightmare, and you would be well fed, and with the minimum of exertion on your part.'

'Your proposal is certainly of interest,' said the lion. 'If I felt I could rely on you – '

'You can be absolutely certain of our good faith,' the animals assured the lion. 'Each day, one of us will come before you as an offering.'

'Somehow, though, it does seem to go against natural law,' said the lion, still not completely sure about the idea. 'Even a superior lion such as myself feels he should exert himself a little for his daily food, whereas under this system . . .'

'But isn't there a divine law,' one of the animals suggested, 'that all creatures should depend on God for sustenance?'

'Yes, well, put like that,' the lion considered for a few moments longer, then, 'all right, I'll give it a try. But see to it, now, that I get a regular, fat and juicy supply, or it will be even worse for you all than it is now.'

So, every day the animals drew lots. The luckless one reported to the lion and sacrificed himself for the sake of the rest who were able to enjoy the peaceful valley once more – at least on a day-to-day basis.

THE LION AND THE HARE

The day came when the lot fell on the hare. However, instead of going off to his fate, the hare stayed where he was and cried out: 'How long are we going to put up with this?'

The animals drew back in horror. 'What's the matter with you?' they demanded. 'You know what we agreed. All the animals so far have accepted the system and sacrificed themselves. So, hurry off, the lion is waiting. Go on, or it will be the worse for all of us.'

'Friends,' the hare replied, 'I have a plan. If it works, not only will I myself escape death, but so will all of you, and your offspring from this day on.'

'We won't hear of it,' the frightened animals protested. 'You're a hare – don't behave like a conceited ass. Be off, or the lion will start hunting us all over again.'

'I'm sure my plan would work,' the hare insisted with a smile.

The terrified animals fell to shouting at each other, one group yelling, 'We'll hear the plan!', another lot screaming, 'No, no, chase him to the lion's den!' Then they fell to horrified silence, for they noticed that the hare had gone.

By now he was very near the den and could hear the lion tearing up the bushes and earth, and roaring. 'I knew they wouldn't keep it up! They've tricked me! Now they're going to pay for it!'

The hare listened for a few moments longer. Then, panting and sighing, he hopped before the lion.

'Ahah!' the lion growled, 'so you're here at last, are you? How dare you make me wait, I, the king of beasts who have torn oxen limb from limb? Am I now reduced to waiting meekly – for a hare?'

'Mercy, mercy!' cried the hare. 'Oh, what a business I've had getting here. If you would graciously hear me out – '

'You must think I have ass's ears if you expect me to listen to the paltry excuses of a hare!' roared the lion, peering closer. 'And a very poor creature at that. Was I supposed to be satisfied for a whole day with a skinny thing like you?'

'Oh, but that's the point', gasped the hare. 'There were two of us when we set out, me and my brother. We knew just one of us wouldn't be enough.'

'So, where is he, then?' the lion growled.

'I had to leave him, with -er- the other lion.'

'The other lion? Other lion! *What* other lion?'

'But that was what I was going to ask you, Majesty,' said the hare. 'I felt sure you would know all about him.'

'Never heard of him!' roared the lion.

'Well, he's real enough,' replied the hare, 'terrifyingly so. He suddenly jumped out and captured us both. Hands off! I said, we are slaves of the King of Beasts, the lion who rules these parts.'

'Quite right,' said the lion. 'And what did he have to say to that, eh?'

'He – er – forgive me, O king. He laughed.'

'WHAT?'

'King of Beasts! said he. Some decrepit old has-been of a lion, I suppose. Don't mention him in my presence again. Now, I'll have you for breakfast and your companion here for elevenses.'

By this time the lion was beside himself with anger, as the hare went on:

'I begged this – the other lion, Majesty, I implored

him: Before you have breakfast, please, please allow me to see the face of my King once more, at least to warn him all about you. All right, hare, said he, but I'll keep your companion here as hostage, meantime. With that I had to agree', said the hare, 'and so, here I am.'

'I'll tear him to pieces!' yelled the lion in a towering rage. 'Where is this other lion? Take me to him, at once.'

So the hare led the way, with the lion – who, after all the months of rich, lazy living had by now grown fat and breathless – lumbering after him. At last they approached a large hole in the ground. The hare drew back.

'What's the matter?' panted the lion. 'Why do you hesitate?'

The hare shivered. 'He's down there', he whispered. 'I must admit I'm terrified at the thought of seeing him again.'

'How dare you be terrified' growled the lion, 'when I, your king, am here with you? In a few moments, believe me, this other lion of yours will have met his death.'

'Well, all right, then', the hare replied. 'If you'll stay by my side as we peep down, I shall have a little more courage.'

So the lion and the hare approached the hole and peered over the edge into its depths.

And there at the bottom, glaring up at them was the other lion!

'And look', whispered the hare, 'there, beside him is my brother who, if we hadn't been stopped, would have been inside you by now!'

The lion roared in absolute fury. At the same time, down below, the other lion roared back in defiance. The lion crouched and reared up to jump. So did the other lion. With the loudest roar he had ever made the lion lost all caution – and leapt down the hole.

And that, of course, was the end of him. All the animals came out of hiding, dancing and singing, to congratulate the hare on ridding them of their enemy – by getting him to jump to his death, down a well.

The Secret Message

A MERCHANT who was about to journey to India called all his slaves and servants and said to them:

'I am going to bring you each a present back from my travels. Tell me what you would like and I will do my best to bring it for you.' They were all delighted and readily gave suggestions.

Then the merchant turned to his pet parrot, a beautiful bird which he kept imprisoned in a cage.

'And what about you?' he asked. 'What shall I bring you from the land of India?'

'India,' sighed the parrot, 'land of my birth, alas! O my master, all I require is that, if you should see any of my friends and relations on your travels, you remind them of me, caught here by the destiny of Heaven. Tell them I think of them always, and ask if they have any message for me.'

'I will certainly do my best to pass your message to any

parrots I meet', said the merchant. 'And now, farewell'.

He travelled many days through India. Towards the end of his journey, while passing through a plain, he caught sight of several parrots in a tree. He halted, called up to them, and gave the parrots the message from his own parrot at home.

The parrots all listened carefully to what he had to say and all seemed concerned, particularly one of the birds. As soon as the merchant finished, this bird trembled violently, then suddenly stiffened and fell dead at the merchant's feet. The other birds flew round the tree crying piteously and the merchant was considerably distressed.

'This poor bird must have been a friend or relative of the parrot at home', he said, 'and now I have been the means of bringing about its death. I wish I had never spoken. I was very foolish', he said, resuming his journey.

When, at last, the merchant arrived back home, he was greeted with great joy. He opened up his baggage, and there were cries of delight as he gave out the presents.

The parrot waited patiently, but at last cried out:

'Did you deliver my message, O Master? Is there any word for me?'

'I delivered it,' said the merchant, with a sad glance at the parrot, 'but I wish I hadn't. I've regretted it ever since.'

'But what happened?' said the parrot.

'Well, I passed on your message,' said the merchant, 'to a group of parrots who, by their plumage, seemed to be of your species. Alas, one of the birds – she must have known you, I believe, – was so distressed that she fell dead at my feet. I was exceedingly sorry, I can tell you. But it was useless being sorry then. I wish I had never delivered your message, I can tell you.'

The parrot listened gravely to the merchant's story. Then, to the merchant's horror, it too began to tremble. In a few seconds it had stiffened, toppled from its perch and lay dead at the bottom of its cage.

The merchant cried out in absolute despair: 'Alas, alas, my beautiful bird! What a fool I am! I should have known. I should have realised.' In tears he reached into the cage and took out the parrot –

whereupon it suddenly flapped its wings and mounted up to freedom.

Perched on a tree top it called down: 'The parrot in India was not dead, O my former master. By a trick, you see, she was explaining how I might escape my imprisonment.'

One Against Three

A GARDENER, GLANCING into his orchard, saw three thieves there, obviously after his fruit. He looked closer: one appeared to be a lawyer, another a noble, and the third a Sufi – yet each of them was obviously a rascal, intent on stealing his produce.

'Now what shall I do?' said the gardener to himself. 'While I've undoubtedly got right on my side, what's the use of that without the power to enforce it? I'm helpless against the three of them all together – ahah! That gives me an idea . . .'

He went smiling into his orchard and greeted the three with courtesy.

'Good day to you, my friends, and welcome to my orchard,' he cried. 'Phew, it's hot today, isn't it? Sit here, under the shade, good sirs. But wait a moment, it's not very clean under that tree. You must have a rug. Now, where's my servant? Oh, what a nuisance – as usual, nowhere to be found. I wonder,' he said, turning to the Sufi, 'would you do me a favour, and go up to my house and ask them to give you a rug? Ah, thank you, I'm most obliged to you.'

As soon as the Sufi had gone, the gardener turned to the lawyer and the noble.

'What a debt we humble folk have to you great ones of our society,' he said. 'Without lawyers, where would we be? How could we run our affairs? – we couldn't even eat a loaf without guidance. As for nobles, without them for our example the whole of society would decline. But one thing puzzles me: how come you both to be associated with that Sufi fellow? I must say it does surprise me. It was on the tip of my tongue to make an invitation to you – until I saw him, that is, the gluttonous, vile fellow. So, as it is . . .'

'What would have been the invitation?' the two thieves asked.

'Well, such is my gratitude for the way you help us poor humble folk I was going to invite you to stay here for a whole week, entirely at my expense, of course – a poor recompense when I owe my entire existence to you. However . . . I wonder now, why

45

don't you let me drive this Sufi fellow off? He doesn't deserve to be included, surely? He lets the whole tone of the group down.'

The lawyer and the noble readily agreed to the suggestion, and were happy to leave the Sufi to the gardener, who picked up a cudgel and met the Sufi as he came back with the rug.

'So!' he shouted, 'dog that you are, take that! And that! And that! What a disgrace you are! Since when has thieving been part of your faith, eh?'

'Help, help!' cried the Sufi, but his two former companions were deaf to his cries as the cudgel rained down on his head.

'False ones!' howled the Sufi as he staggered off. 'This gardener has beaten me – so now you'd better watch out. The same thing will happen to you –'. But the gardener cut short his warnings with renewed blows and didn't stop until the Sufi had run howling away.

'Phew!' said the gardener, returning to the two under the trees, 'that's got rid of him.' He laid down the rug and invited them to recline. 'Well, now,' he continued, 'the day is yours. What about something to eat and drink, eh? My wife is baking fresh bread and is cooking a goose – we'll have that to begin with. How delighted she will be at entertaining such nobility. She's a silly girl but nothing would gladden her heart more than to meet a noble of the land. I wonder, sir, if you would consent to approach the house and give the order for the food to be brought out? You have but to command – my house is yours.'

'Certainly, my dear fellow,' said the noble obligingly, and off he went.

As soon as he was out of earshot, the gardener sniffed. 'Anyone can see he's not a noble,' he declared. 'You're obviously a lawyer, and a very learned one at that, but this fellow, who does he think he's kidding? Our country is full of base-born rascals claiming to be nobles – the land is over-run by them – but as soon as one starts enquiring into their parentage, what scandals are uncovered then, eh? Well, he didn't take me in, and I'm certain you aren't fooled either.'

'You're quite right,' said the lawyer.

'Well, then,' said the gardener, picking up the cudgel, 'let's see him out of the way, and then we can enjoy ourselves in peace.'

Off he went through the trees where he met the noble returning from the house.

'You big ass!' he cried, raining down blow after blow of his cudgel. 'How did you hope to pass yourself off as a noble? What an insult! From which noble family did you inherit the art of trickery, well?'

'Ow! Ouch!' howled the noble and shouted to the lawyer, 'why are you sitting there? What happened to our plan? Ow! Ow! Traitor! Watch out for yourself, then, if this crafty gardener is the companion you've chosen instead of me. Yow! Mercy! Mercy! I'm off ...!'

And he too, fled, groaning in agony.

'Now, finally, as for *you*!' the gardener yelled triumphantly, turning and descending furiously on the lawyer. 'Lawyer, indeed! I wouldn't insult fools by calling you one. Take that! And that! Was it your legal opinion, then, that you could come into my garden without so much as a by-your-leave? Away with you! Off you go!'

'Enough, enough, have mercy!' screamed the lawyer, staggering under the blows. 'You've beaten us all. Lawyer or not, I'm certainly suffering - ouch! -

a just penalty for one that allows himself - yow! - to be parted from his friends!'

Appointment
With Death

*... and other tales of fate,
destiny and the inevitable*

Appointment With Death

*O*NE OF King Solomon's nobles came into his presence shuddering, white-faced and with his lips blue with terror.

'My friend', said the King, 'what has happened?'

'I've just met Azrael, the Angel of Death, as I crossed the forecourt', the noble gasped. 'It must mean that my end is near.'

King Solomon smiled. 'You would not be alive to tell me this', he said, 'if it meant that. No, rest assured, my friend. It is not common knowledge, but I regularly meet and talk with Azrael, and we are to meet today in fact. You must have met him as he was on his way here.'

But the noble was unconvinced.

'Azrael looked so keenly at me', he shuddered. 'He seemed to recognise me. I am sure he would have spoken to me if I had not hurried away. Woe is me! What shall I do? O, what shall I do?'

'I'm certain you need not fear' the King persisted. 'But if I can help you in any way, you have but to command me and I will do all in my power.'

'Well', said the noble, 'is it true that you have power over the winds?'

'It is.'

'Could you order them to carry me away, far from here - to India, even?'

'I can, and will' said Solomon. At once, the winds swirled through the palace, lifted the terrified noble up and away to distant India.

Not long after this, Azrael, Angel of Death, entered the presence of the King.

'Greetings, Azrael', said Solomon. 'You certainly startled one of my nobles just now. He caught a glimpse of you as you entered the palace.'

'He could not have been more surprised than I was myself', said Azrael. 'I was astonished to see him *here*. You see, this afternoon I have an appointment with him - in India.'

Doctor, It's Like This . . .

'I'M GETTING a lot of headaches,' said the old man to his doctor.

'They are due to your age,' said the doctor.

'And spots before my eyes – '

'They are to be expected in one of your age.'

'My back is giving me agony.'

'Well, that's not surprising at your age.'

'And I have to be careful what I eat or – '

'Or you get tummy-ache. It's due to your age, you see.'

'As for my breathing, oh dear.'

'Asthma, yes, yes – all part of the hundred and one ailments you can expect at your age.'

The old man lost his temper. 'Age, age, age! Is that all you can say, you fool? Have you gone all the way through medical school, just to say, It's age, to every one of my complaints? Don't you know there's a God-given cure for every illness?'

The doctor remained calm. This made the old man worse. He jumped up, red in the face. 'Stupid ass!' he cried. 'No wonder you've remained a lowly doctor. It's the only place for one of your poor ability and feeble wits. What a diagnosis – age, age, age!'

The doctor sighed. 'Well', he sighed, 'I need hardly add, then, that even your bad temper is also due to – er – the same complaint.'

Decreed by God

'*I* COULDN'T help it,' said the thief to the magistrate. 'What I did was decreed by God.'

'My dear friend,' said the magistrate, 'what I shall do is also decreed by Him. Off you go to prison.'

The Destiny of the Hoopoe Bird

*O*NCE, WHEN KING SOLOMON had pitched his tent, all the birds of the air came to pay homage. One by one they flew into his presence, discovering with delight that he could understand and speak to them in their own language. Each of the birds revealed its secret knowledge and skills, seeking to serve him.

At length, Solomon turned to a hoopoe bird locked in a cage.

'O King,' said the hoopoe,' I have only one talent, a poor one, and it can be told briefly.'

'Tell me what it is,' said Solomon.

'When I have flown as high as my wings can take me,' the bird replied, 'from that height I can look down on the earth and see exactly where water is to be found, how deep it is, whether or not it is clear and good, and if it gushes from clay or rock. A poor talent, but it could come in useful when your army is marching through desert places.'

'Useful indeed!' Solomon replied, rising to release him. 'What a good friend you would be on my expeditions.'

At this, an envious crow hopped into the King's presence. 'He's a liar,' said the crow. 'If the hoopoe is as clear-sighted as all that, how come he didn't catch sight of the snare that trapped him? Or did he go into that cage just for the fun of it?'

Solomon turned to the hoopoe. 'What have you to say to that, my friend? Are you merely a braggart and a liar?'

'I have told you the truth, Great King,' the hoopoe replied, 'but, as for the crow, do not listen to him. He is an unbeliever, else he would surely know that all wisdom, all intelligence and skill are of no use at all when Destiny intervenes.'

Both in the Same Boat

. . . and other stories about learning, wisdom and common sense

Both in the Same Boat

*A*S THE PROFESSOR of literature was getting into the boat he said to the boatman: 'Tell me, my good man, have you ever studied grammar?'

'No, sir', the boatman replied.

'Alas', said the professor loftily, 'what a pity. Without such knowledge you've wasted half your life.'

The boat set off. Not long after, a storm blew up. The boat was caught in a whirlpool.

The boatman shouted above the chaos: 'Tell me, sir, have you ever learned to swim?'

'No, no!' the professor cried.

'Alas', the boatman replied, 'what a pity. Without such knowledge you've wasted *all* your life!'

A Sack Full of Sand

*A*N ARAB was loading his camel with two sacks when he fell into conversation with a talkative philosopher. The philosopher gabbled on about every subject under the sun, enquiring closely into the Arab's country and circumstances. He even asked what he had in his sacks.

'Why', said the Arab, 'this one's full of grain, and the one on the other side is full of sand.'

'Sand?' said the philosopher. 'Why do you burden your camel with a sack of sand?'

'Oh, it's just to balance the sack of wheat.'

'But surely', the philosopher laughed, 'you could put half the wheat in one sack and half in the other? You will still get the balance and the camel only half the load.'

The Arab gaped in admiration.

'I never thought of that', he said. 'What a clever

man you are. And yet', he continued, looking at him more closely, 'here you are in rags, journeying on foot. What's the reason for it? With your wits you are obviously a ruler in disguise or at the very least, a vizier.'

'I'm neither' replied the philosopher. 'Look at me carefully; this is no disguise.'

'Oh come', said the Arab, 'you can rely on my discretion if you are in hiding for some reason. Tell me, how many camels to you own, how many oxen?'

'No camels, no oxen', said the philosopher. 'Stop mocking me.'

'A shopkeeper, then, that's what you are, isn't it so? Have I guessed it? What do you deal in? What do you sell in your shop?'

'I haven't got a shop', cried the philosopher. 'I don't even have a roof over my head!'

'Ahah!' smiled the Arab, 'now I have it! All your wealth is in gold, hidden away. You've rejected possessions, preferring the freedom of a wanderer. Your riches are wisdom, your pearls are those of knowledge and understanding – '

'Stop! Stop! It's not true', shouted the philosopher.
'I'm penniless – I don't have enough even for a meal
tonight. Look, I don't have any shoes, and even my
rags are threadbare. I'm a wandering beggar, going
wherever there's a possibility of half a loaf. For all
my wisdom and cleverness, the result is just a
headache.'

'Then be off with you!' said the Arab. 'It's obvious
that a man with your cleverness and wisdom, yet in
the condition you are in, must be cursed by bad
luck and I don't want any of it spreading to me!
Whichever direction you go', he said, 'I'll go in the
other. And what's more', he added, patting his
camel, 'I'll stick to my one sack of wheat and one
sack of sand!'

Just Like Home

*J*UHI AND HIS father passed an open coffin before which a boy was crying.

'O, Father,' the distraught boy sobbed over the body, 'they are taking you to a narrow and miserable place where there are no carpets or comforts of any kind, no lamps in the evening, no food at mealtimes, where the doors have come away from the hinges, and the roof is leaking, where there are no friends and no neighbours. How can you, whom we all loved, go to that dark and murky hole, that pitiless house, and that narrow room which rarely sees the light of day?'

'Good gracious, Papa,' whispered Juhi, 'are they bringing the corpse to our house, then?'

A Chat at Midnight

'*G*ET UP, GET up!'

'Wha – what's that? Who – ?'

'You can't lie there. It's past twelve of the clock. What have you been drinking?'

'Whatever was in this bottle, Inspector.'

'The bottle's empty. What was in it?'

'Whatever it was I drank – '

'I'm, taking you off to prison. You're drunk. Follow me.'

'Heaven help me! Follow you? Do you think I would be lying here, talking to you, Inspector, if I could do that?'

The Ambitious Ant

SO, YOU MET an ant who told you that it hoped one day to become as great as King Solomon.

But why did you laugh?

Everything you have become – your skill, your craft, your knowledge, your ability – was it not once just an idea as small as that ant?

The Royal Way

THE KING WAS on his way to the mosque to pray. Before him went his guards with whips and cudgels.

'Out of the way!' they shouted, hitting out at whoever was unfortunate enough to be in the King's path, cracking the head of one, tearing the clothes of another.

One poor fellow, who had done no harm, got more than most of the blows. Bruised and bloody, he turned to the King and cried:

'Majesty! If this is the good you do on the way to the mosque, I dread to think what sins you'll confess when you actually get there!'

The Call to Prayer

*A*T DAWN THE Amir roused his slave. 'Up, Sungar, rouse yourself! I feel like going to the hot springs for a bathe. Hurry! Get the towels, get the soap.'

Sungar obeyed, got the soap and towels, and they set off together. On the way they passed the mosque and at that moment there came the call to prayer. Now Sungar, unlike his master, was a devout believer. He loved the ritual of prayer and wished his master did, too.

'O, my master,' he begged, 'give me leave to say my prayers. If you yourself do not want to pray, would you mind waiting here on this bench for me?'

The Amir reluctantly agreed. Sungar joined the people inside.

At last the prayers were over. The people came out – all except Sungar.

'What's keeping him?' muttered the Amir fretfully.

'I know he likes praying, but there is a limit.' He went on waiting. Eventually he called out:

'Hey, Sungar!'

'Yes, master?' came the response from within.

'Why don't you come out? What's keeping you in there?'

'O, my master, have patience, I beg. I will be as quick as I can.'

There followed another long wait. The Amir grew angry, and called again: 'There is no-one left in the mosque but you, Sungar. Answer me! Who, then, is keeping you there?'

'O, my master, that same one who prevents your coming in, he it is who prevents my coming out!'

Boo!

'*BOGIES?*' ANSWERED THE mother to her child who had cried out in the night. 'Don't be afraid of *them*, my dear. Whenever you think you see one – in a nightmare or in a graveyard or some such place – rush at it boldly and it will soon turn tail.'

'But suppose,' the child replied, 'that what you have just said to me is exactly what the bogie's mother says to *it*?'

Three Words from a Magic Bird

*... ten tales of fools
and what happened to them*

Three Words from a Magic Bird

*B*Y CUNNING AND a carefully set trap, a man once caught a bird. To his surprise, when he was about to kill and eat it, the bird spoke to him.

'My dear sir,' it said, 'you've eaten sheep and even oxen in your time, and have risen from the table still hungry, so it's hardly likely that you'll get any satisfaction out of what little flesh is on my bones. However, if you will set me free I will be able to give you three wise sayings which will be of great value to you. What do you say?'

The astonished man agreed.

'Very well, then,' said the bird. 'Listen carefully. The first saying I will give you as soon as you open your hand. The second I will give you from your own rooftop, and the third from that tree over there. If you heed what I say you will reap a fortune. So, now, if you're ready ... ?'

The man opened his hand.

'Thank you,' said the bird. 'Now, this is the first saying: If what you hear is obvious nonsense, don't believe it, whoever tells it to you.'

Having said this, the bird quickly flew up to the roof. 'Here is the second saying,' it cried. 'Don't grieve over what is past, forget it.' Then the bird continued: 'I have to tell you now that I have swallowed a precious pearl, fully ten dirams in weight, a pearl that would have brought wealth and prosperity to you and your descendants for generations to come. But, by releasing me, you have lost it!'

At this the man cried aloud, wailing piteously, tearing his clothes in anguish and regret.

'Come, come,' the bird called down. 'What is the point of my giving you these wise sayings if you don't heed them? Was not my second saying, just now, that you should not regret what is past? Do stop this noise, therefore. And you paid as little heed to my first saying as you did to the second.'

'How so?' sobbed the man.

'Did I not tell you not to believe obvious nonsense?

I myself weigh only a couple of dirams. You know that, for you have held me in your hand. How then could I have, concealed within me, a pearl weighing ten dirams?'

'O, of course, of course', cried the relieved man. 'So now, O wise bird, give me the third saying.'

The bird flew to the tree.

'Knowing what use you have made of my first two sayings', said the bird, 'I have decided that my third will also be wasted on you. And so, farewell.'

And away it flew.

The Impossible Lion

THE PEOPLE OF Kaswin have a custom of having themselves tattooed with blue figures and symbols as a magic protection against harm.

Once, a man of Kaswin went to a barber to have the tattooing done. 'I want a really artistic job', he said.

'Valiant one, it shall be a masterpiece', the barber replied. 'Now, what sort of thing do you want?'

'I want the figure of a ferocious lion. Leo is my sign, you see, and this will be a sign of my courage in battle. Now, barber excel yourself in artistry. Use your best needles, and do not spare the blue dye, eh?'

'I understand perfectly, sir. Now, where would you like it?'

'Just here, on my shoulder blade.'

'Right, sir, if you'll just sit here?' The barber prepared his implements.

But as soon as the needle went in, the man let out a howl of pain.

'Yowwwww! What are you doing? You're killing me!'

'You asked for a lion – '

'Yes, I know, I know – but what part of the lion was that?'

'I was beginning, sir, with the tail.'

'Forget it, man. I'll do without the tail. Just get on with the rest of it.'

The barber set to work on another part of the man's shoulder.

'Yowwwww! What part of the lion is that?'

'The first of the ears, my dear sir.'

'Leave them out, leave them out. This lion will have to be deaf. This is agony. Well, get on with rest of it.'

But as soon as the barber inserted a needle in another part of the man's shoulder, there was a further agonised scream and a demand to know which part of the lion's anatomy was being tattooed.

'This is the belly, sir.'

'Let it do without one', cried the man. 'I've certainly had my belly-full of this, I can tell you. Well, get on with the rest of it!'

But the barber, exasperated, threw down his needle.

'Nay, sir', he replied, 'whoever saw a lion without a tail, ears or a belly? If God himself cannot make such a creature, how do you expect me to tattoo it? Off you go! Next, please . . .'

The Sick Visitor

A MESSAGE WAS brought to a deaf man that a neighbour had fallen ill.

'Oh dear,' said the deaf man, 'I suppose I shall have to go and visit him. But it's not much use, really. I'm as deaf as a post, so conversation is difficult, to say the least. And, as he's ill, his voice will be weak and I shan't hear a word. Still, there's no escaping; one must visit the sick.'

On the way, he carried on muttering to himself.

'I shall have to think of some sort of reply when I see his lips moving. I shall have to guess. I suppose it shouldn't be too difficult really . . .

'I will begin by saying, How are you, my poor friend? And then, no doubt he'll reply: I'm fine, or I'm on the mend. Then all I need say is:

'Thanks be to God. What medicines are you taking?'

'He'll no doubt reply: Some sherbet, or kidney bean soup.

'I could then say: Well, I hope it restores you to full health. Which doctor is attending you?

'He'll say: So-and-so.

'Ahah! I'll reply. I've heard he's very good. Oh, you'll soon be back to full strength.'

So, having worked all this out, the deaf visitor arrived at the house of the sick man and was shown into his room.

'How are you, my poor friend?' he cried.

'I'm at the point of death,' came the reply.

'Thanks be to God,' said the deaf man. 'I'm so pleased. Do tell me, what medicines are you taking?'

'Poison!' groaned the invalid.

'Excellent!' said his visitor. 'I'm sure it will restore you to full health. And which doctor is attending you?'

'Azrael, the angel of death,' groaned the exasperated man.

'Oh he's good, very good. You'll soon be back on your feet, dear friend. Well, now I must be going. God be with you!'

'Well, that seemed to go all right,' he said as he set
off back to his home.

The Ass is Gone!

A SUFI AND his servant were made welcome at a very poor monastery. The Sufi went with his servant and himself saw to it that the ass had water and fodder. Then he joined the monks.

Now, though the monks had welcomed their visitor they were in fact so poor that they had nothing to give him. And such was their poverty that it led them to lose their sense of right and wrong. They overpowered and tied up the servant, then took the ass to market and sold it. With the money they bought food of all kinds, together with many candles.

'Tonight we'll celebrate!' they cried. 'We'll have enough to eat, and more – an end to all this fasting! – and there will be music and dancing. We have a guest to entertain, so let's seize this opportunity and do it properly!'

The Sufi was flattered by the festivities put on in his honour and, though he was tired, he appreciated that it would be impolite not to join in. 'While there is such an opportunity as this', he thought, 'it would be foolish not to make merry.'

So, they all fell to and ate their fill. The monastery was aglow with light, and towards the end of the meal the musicians struck up.

The monks rose and danced, waving their hands and stamping their feet in their excitement. Soon, the Sufi was among them, as lost as they were in the ecstasy of song and dance.

When the dance ended, a solitary voice was heard to cry out: 'The ass is gone!'

At this the minstrels quickly struck up again – and this time the singer intoned, to a wailing accompaniment:

'The ass is gone, the ass is gone.'

'The ass is gone, the ass is gone', chanted the monks with great feeling, and though the Sufi thought these words were strange to be singing he was soon caught up again in the fervour of the song, and sang more loudly than any in the company:

'The ass is gone, the ass is gone!'

At dawn, the Sufi awoke to find himself in a deserted monastery. A little surprised, he collected his baggage and took it out to the stable. 'They'll all have gone on a pilgrimage, I suppose,' he said. 'I'll soon catch up with them.'

But the stable, too, was deserted. 'Ah, the servant will have taken my ass to water,' he said. 'I remember it drank little last night.'

But the servant returned alone.

'Where is the ass?' cried the Sufi.

'Don't be a fool, old man,' the servant replied.

'But I left it in your care!' the Sufi shouted. 'What do you mean by this? Where is the ass? I insist on your returning it to me this instant. What an insolent fellow you are. Come along now, or have I to call the police?'

'Have you completely forgotten last night?' the servant shouted back. 'What did you expect me to do? Those monks overpowered me. I protested loudly but they got so angry that I was afraid for my life. They tied me up, then took the ass and sold it.'

'But why, why didn't you come and tell me?'

'I did, I did!' the servant protested. 'The ass is gone! I cried when at last I was able to free myself and make myself heard. But you seemed so delighted, singing and repeating "The ass is gone!" louder and more excitedly than everyone else – why, I felt sure you knew all about it!'

Spoilt Prayers

*F*OUR MEN WENT early into a mosque to pray, all agreeing to be silent in the intensity of their worship as they lay prostrate on the ground.

But then, suddenly, when the muezzin came to call worshippers to prayer, one of the men let slip:

'What, is it that time already?'

'Hey!' said the second man without thinking, 'you have spoken. Your prayer is null and void.'

'Fool!' cried the third to the second, 'so is yours, if that's the case.'

'Praise God', cried the fourth, 'that *I* haven't fallen into the pit of error like these three!'

The Not So Clever Bird

*T*HE BIRD-CATCHER LAID a trap with tempting grains of wheat. Disguising himself with greenery and flowers, he settled down in the bushes to wait.

Along came a little bird. It ignored the grain and hopped up to the man.

'What's the idea?' it said. 'What are you doing there, dressed up in leaves and flowers? Explain yourself.'

'Er . . . well, it's like this,' said the bird-catcher, taken by surprise, 'I'm a holy man who believes in living simply, all the while in touch with nature.'

'How did you come by this belief?' the bird demanded.

'It all began,' said the man, thinking quickly, 'yes, it all began when my dear friend and neighbour died suddenly. What a shock it gave me. I realised that it could easily happen to me, and that I was quite unprepared to meet my God. So, I sold my business, turned my back on all my relations and friends, and, well, here I am, preparing myself for the grave.'

'I hope you know what you're doing,' said the bird. 'Our faith insists that the believer does not withdraw from the world – on the contrary it demands that we join in public worship and do battle daily with evil in the day-to-day affairs of the world, that we bear its troubles, and help all in need.'

'That's true,' said the man. 'However . . .' and the whole morning was spent in discussion. Man and bird debated the advantages and disadvantages of the way of life that the bird-catcher had supposedly put forward.

Then – at last – the bird noticed the grains of wheat.

'And what's this?' it asked.

'Oh . . . Oh that,' said the man. 'Well, it happens to belong to an orphan who lives nearby. Poor child, it's the only property he possesses. He doesn't even have a guardian, so when he asked if I would look after it for him, what else could I do?'

'I feel quite hungry after all our discussion,' said the bird, eying the grain. 'Would you mind if I ate just a bit of it?'

'You must judge that for yourself,' replied the man. 'A bird of your learning will know, I'm sure, that if you eat when you're not hungry, that's a sin. And even if you are hungry, it's better to abstain. But then, if you must eat, you ought at least to pay.'

The bird thought about, looked again at the grain, and gave in. It dived at the grain – and found itself in the trap. It gave a loud cry of despair.

'This is what comes of talking to holy men!'

'Not at all,' said the bird-catcher. 'It is what comes of robbing orphans!'

Double-Crossed

A MAN, LOST in thought, was leading his ram on a rope. A thief came up behind him, cut the rope and ran off with the ram. Quite a while later the man came to – and loud were his cries as he ran here and there. But, of course, no-one had seen his ram.

In a little while he came to a well near which a man was wailing piteously:

'Alas, alas, what shall I do now?'

'What's the matter?' asked the first man.

'My purse – I've just dropped it down the well. If only I could find someone to go down there and get it out, why, I'd give him a fifth part of what is in it.'

'And what is in it?' asked the man.

'A hundred dinars.'

A hundred dinars! thought the man. That means

that, if I recover his purse, I'll end up with twenty dinars – worth ten rams at least!

'I'll get it!' he cried. He took off all his clothes and dived in.

And the thief ran off with his clothes.

The Turk and the Tailor

*O*NE NIGHT a story-teller delighted his listeners with tales about the wickedness of tailors, how they filched bits of cloth from the pieces brought to them to be made up, even as the owners looked on. He had a whole host of such stories and the laughter was loud as tale followed tale of the trickery of tailors.

However, among his listeners was a Turk who grew more and more annoyed as the tales unfolded. At last he could bear it no longer.

'These tales are a gross insult to all the tailors in the kingdom,' he shouted. 'I don't believe any of them. If there's the slightest evidence of this sort of thing going on, you tell me the name of the tailor. Go on, give me the name of the biggest expert in your city at this sort of fraud!'

'I can think of many,' the story-teller replied, 'but if it's the expert you want, well, that must be a tailor called Piri Shush.'

'Right', said the Turk, 'I'm willing to bet that he couldn't steal even an inch of thread in my presence.'

The rest of the audience shook their heads. 'Don't be rash', said one. 'We all know this tailor. He's hoodwinked cleverer men than you.'

'Don't risk your bet', said another. 'You're bound to lose.'

But this merely made the Turk even more angry and more determined.

'I'll take you all on', he cried. 'Look, here is my horse. I'll give this tailor my horse if he steals any cloth of mine. But if he cannot rob me, you will all club together to give me another horse as fine as this one.'

And they all agreed.

That night the Turk could not sleep. In his imagination he was watching the fingers of the tailor at work on his cloth. In the morning he bought a piece of rich satin, and sought out the shop of Piri Sush.

The tailor sprang from his seat with a smile of

welcome and a sincere enquiry as to the health of
the Turk. His greeting was so genuine that the Turk
immediately warmed to him.

'And now, what can I do for you?' Piri Shush asked.
The Turk unrolled the cloth.

'Stamboul Satin!' the tailor exclaimed. 'What
richness, what quality!'

'I would like you to make me a coat', the Turk said.

'It will be an honour.'

'At the top, here, I should like it to be tight –'

'To show off your admirable figure.'

'And below, here, it should be wide –'

'So as not to hamper your athletic legs in battle. Oh,
I can see this coat already, my dear sir. This is
indeed a pleasure', exclaimed the tailor. He quickly
measured the Turk, begged him to be seated, ran his
hands lovingly over the satin, and took out his
scissors. As he did so, his tongue never stopped
wagging. Piri Shush had a fund of funny stories –
misers, chieftains, slaves – all their tricks and
accidents came into his tales.

Soon the Turk was rocking with laughter. He threw back his head and closed his streaming eyes, shrieking with mirth.

And with a quiet snip the tailor cut off a piece of satin and slipped it under the counter.

'More, more,' cried the Turk. And the tailor was delighted to oblige. The next joke so delighted the Turk that he fell on his back in an explosion of mirth – and another bit of satin disappeared.

'Oh, go on, go on!' the Turk entreated. 'Do you know any more? Tell me, tell me, I beg of you.'

The next jokes were even better. The Turk abandoned all control. Gasping with laughter, he rocked to and fro, his eyes shut in ecstasy.

And snip, snip, more and more of the satin disappeared.

'Oh, where do you get them? Do you know any more?' the Turk pleaded. He was insatiable – and the satin grew less and less.

At last, after the umpteenth demand for jokes, even the rascal of a tailor had to give up, and take pity on the Turk.

'You poor fool,' he cried, 'you're defrauding yourself.
Don't you understand? If I tell you any more,
there'll be no coat left for you to get into!'

The Treasure-Seeker

A MAN OF Baghdad, who was left a lot of money, squandered it all and quickly found himself penniless. Without money, goods, house or home he cried to God:

'Lord, you gave me all this. Now it is gone. I beg you, give me more, or send death to relieve me of my misery.'

That night he had a dream. A voice said to him: 'Go to Cairo, the City of Good Fortune. There your wealth will be restored.'

Immediately the man got up and set off. Having no money, he had to walk all the way, and it was only after many weary days that he arrived. But his spirit lightened as he entered the gate. However, he was now absolutely destitute, in rags, and starving. He thought of begging, but shame held him back.

'I'll wait till nightfall,' he told himself. 'It will be easier to beg in the dark.'

But in the darkness he found it no easier. 'Try here', his hunger urged him, but, as his hand stretched to knock at the door, shame drew it back. So he wandered half the night through the black streets.

Now, it so happened at that time that the people of the area had been suffering from many thieves and burglars. There had been loud outcries and complaints that the police were slipping up, so much so that the Caliph himself intervened.

'I want this thieving stopped', he told the Chief of Police. 'Pounce on anyone suspicious and, if you find evidence of burglary, cut off his head – even if it is a relative of mine. See to it, then. It's because you have been slack and lenient that all this crime is starting up again. They're even saying that some of your men are taking bribes. It's all got to stop – and quickly!'

The threats were passed on to his men by the Chief of Police, and the night patrols were warned of the consequences if thieves weren't quickly rounded up.

It was one of these newly vigilant night patrol men who spotted the destitute traveller from Baghdad – and pounced. He rained down blows on the poor man's head so that his shrieks were heard for streets around.

'Mercy!' cried the man in his agony. 'No more! Give me but a moment. Let me explain, I beg!'

'Well,' said the night patrol men, 'all right, then. I can tell you're not from these parts. However, your story had better be a good one, I warn you. We police are under attack for not stopping this crime wave, and you are certainly behaving very suspiciously. So, now, confess. What are you up to, and who are your associates in crime?'

'I'm not a criminal' cried the man. 'I'm a stranger here. I'm a Baghdad man' – and he poured out his story, how he had squandered his money and goods, had cried to God, and dreamed that his wealth would be restored in Cairo. He was obviously so sincere that the night patrol man believed him and relaxed.

'Well, I can see you're not a thief,' he said, 'just a silly fool. Fancy coming all this way because of a dream! You must be mad. Everyone has dreams of that sort. Why, I myself was dreaming such stuff only last night. Only my voice told me to go to Baghdad – where you come from! But do you think I shall trail to Baghdad for hidden treasure because of a dream? Not likely! Even though my voice actually told me the name of the street. What was it, let me try to remember. Oh, yes it was – ' and he named the very street in which the poor man had lived.

'And the place', the night patrol man went on, correctly describing the house where the poor man had lived.

'And the very spot: under the floor-board of the second room. What treasure is hidden *there*, I can tell you, my friend. But you won't catch *me* budging one step from here. It's all a fantasy, that's why! Well, now, be off with you, foolish man, and don't let me catch you hanging around here again. I shan't be so lenient next time.'

The poor man did not need telling twice! In an ecstasy of joy he silently sent aloft a thousand thankful prayers to God. 'A fool, am I?' he cried to the night patrol man. 'I may be a fool, but I'm a lucky one. And what a miracle it is that neither of us responded in the same way to our dreams!'

So saying, the poor man set off back to Baghdad, all the way praising God. 'What wisdom the Lord has', he sang on the journey. 'I was a fool, so he sent me on a fool's errand. I was sitting on the object of my desire, but I could find it only by going as far away from it as possible!'

Thus musing and rejoicing, the man eventually
arrived at the house in Baghdad. There he soon
discovered the treasure which God, by his grace,
had restored to him.

Beauty Treatment

'*O*PEN UP IMMEDIATELY!' CRIED the elderly man.

'Sorry,' said the barber, 'you're too late.'

'Impossible! I must get something done at once about my beard.'

'I can't help you.'

'You must help me, you must. I need all the white hairs taken out.'

'I've an urgent business appointment.'

'Just the white hairs in my beard, that's all. I've chosen a young bride. The wedding is any minute!'

Exasperated, the barber opened the door, sat the old man in his chair and cut off all his beard.

'There! That's all I have time for. Now *you* sort out the white hairs from the black.'

Up a Pear Tree!

*. . . and more stories of
quick-wittedness and
thinking ahead*

Up a Pear Tree!

*S*HE WAS UNDER a pear tree in a shady orchard in the arms of her lover.

'Doesn't your husband have even the slightest notion of what we're up to?' asked the lover.

The woman laughed. 'Him? He's a fool. I'm always pulling the wool over his eyes. Why, I bet I could wangle it that he actually sees us embracing like this, and still does nothing about it.'

'Go on! I know you're clever, but – '

'Here he comes. Hide in the bushes, and I'll show you.'

When the lover was hidden, the woman called: 'Dear one?'

'What is it, my love?' answered the husband.

'Darling, I'm going to climb our pear tree to pick some of the more succulent fruit.'

'O, very well, my sweet. I'll sit here in the shade.'

The woman began climbing the tree. About half way up she stopped climbing and began to cry aloud.

'O, my husband, what a deceiver you are!'

'What do you mean, my angel?'

'Who is that woman you have with you?'

'There is no-one, my love.'

'Stop kissing her! Take your arms away from her, this instant! Alas, to think it has come to this!'

'Are you mad, my darling? I'm alone here!'

'Liar, I can see you both clearly.'

'But I assure you – '

'It must be this tree, then. It gives one delusions.'

'Yes, of course, that must be the explanation. Do come down and see.'

So, the wife came down and pretended to be astonished that her husband was alone.

'I can hardly believe my eyes. Husband, you'd better climb up and see if the tree has any effect on you.'

So the poor husband went up the pear tree.

'Out you come!' laughed the wife, pulling her lover from the bushes and embracing him ardently.

'Here, who's that you have with you?' the husband called from the tree.

'There's no-one here but myself!' the wife called up.

'That man – he has his arms round you – '

'Nonsense!'

'And now you're kissing him!'

'Impossible! What a tree that is, husband, don't you agree? Stay up there for a bit, and let's see how long the illusion lasts.'

Your Money Or . . .

A MURDEROUS ROBBER gang descended on the village, dragged out a couple of the most important men, tied one of them up and prepared to kill him.

'Thieves!' the man cried. 'Why do you want my blood? Why kill me? What's the point? I've no gold, nothing of value at all. I live in poverty.'

'We're going to kill *you*,' said the robber chief, 'as an example to your colleague here of what will happen to *him* if he doesn't tell where his gold is hidden.'

'But he is poorer than I am!' the man cried.

'Not so,' the second man hastily put in. 'He's just pretending to be poor. He's got plenty of gold stashed away.'

'Well, let's not argue the matter,' said the first man. 'But since it seems we might both be of equal value, kill *him* so that *I* will be terrified into revealing my gold!'

Seeing it Through

A MAN ONCE came to a goldsmith and said: 'Please lend me your scales. I want to weigh this gold of mine.'

'Sorry, but I don't have a sieve,' said the goldsmith.

'I didn't ask for a sieve,' said the man. 'I asked for scales. Stop fooling, I've no time to waste.'

'I don't have a broom, either, old man.'

'Enough, enough! Why this pretending to be deaf? Or have you gone mad?'

'No, I haven't,' said the goldsmith. 'Nor am I deaf. I heard quite clearly what you said. I'd better explain. It's like this: you asked for scales, but I looked at you, an elderly man and your hands shaking as well. And I looked at your gold, all tiny fillings. And I thought: He's bound to drop some of that out of the scales. Then he'll say: Sir, could I have a broom to sweep up my gold? Now, my floor is dirty, so I knew you would sweep up the dirt with the gold, and that next you would be asking: Could I have a sieve to sift out my gold? Well, now, as I've neither broom nor sieve, don't you think you'd better find another goldsmith?'

Cries in the Morning

*T*HE WATCHMAN FELL asleep and, while he was snoring, thieves made off with everything.

At dawn, when the caravanners woke, there were loud outcries: 'Where is the luggage?', 'Where are the camels?', 'Where is the money?'

'Watchman!' they cried, 'what happened? Explain yourself, man!'

'Oh, oh, they jumped on me – thieves – before I realised. They were off before I could do anything.'

'But surely you could have done *something*. There isn't a scratch on you. Didn't you make even an attempt to stop them?'

'They were a fierce band, armed to the teeth – hundreds of them. And just the one of me.'

'But surely you could have given a shout? You could have roused us. That's the *least* you could have done – a few shouts. What do we pay you for?'

'Oh, yes, well, I was going to call out, see, when the chief of the thieves produced a knife and said: One squeak out of you and you've had it. Well, imagine, I was terror-struck, speechless, couldn't shout a thing at that moment. But now that they've gone, here's what you pay me for: Help! Robbers! Help! Thieves, thieves! Help!'

The Beast in the Barn

*... stories about first impressions,
judgment, and seeing things
as they really are*

The Beast in the Barn

T HERE WAS GREAT excitement in the village. News had come that some travelling showmen from India were on the way, bringing with them a beast from their country. The head man of the village said he had heard of the name of the beast but couldn't for the life of him remember what it was for the moment. Anyway, he was sure he'd never seen one whatever it was and that was all he could say. The villagers became wild with curiosity.

They waited all day. Night fell, and still the showmen had not arrived. It was pitch dark by the time they did, and nothing could be seen of the beast, which was locked up in a barn, ready to be shown next day.

But four men couldn't sleep, and decided they could not wait till morning. When all was quiet they crept to the barn in the darkness, not daring to bring a lamp or a candle in case they were discovered.

They hoisted themselves up to a window and peered in, but could see nothing. So they opened the window and climbed through. Greatly daring they each began to feel for the animal.

'Goodness!'

'Well, well!'

'So that's it!'

'Magnificent!'

They sighed in wonder at what their hands told them, and when they came out they discussed the beast eagerly.

'It's like a giant water-pipe,' said one.

'Rubbish!' said the second. 'It's more like an enormous fan.'

'You're both wrong,' said the third. 'What I felt was a pillar of great width and height.'

'A pillar? Nonsense!' said the fourth. 'It can only be described as something like a high throne.'

So they argued for the rest of the night – but the argument was not settled until the morning, when the beast was put on display. Then the four men, who had felt the trunk, the ear, the leg and the back of the animal, saw that they had all been right.

But only after they put all the bits together did they know what the elephant was really like.

A Work of Art

*T*HE SULTAN LIKED to have artists
around him and loved the paintings they
produced. But what an argumentative lot the
painters were!

'Undoubtedly, *we* are the superior artists', boasted
the Chinese

'Not at all', claimed the Greeks. 'No-one can excel *us*
in our power to reproduce what we see.'

'Well, well, let's put it to the test', said the Sultan.
'We'll have a competition. Look, here's an old room
with dirty walls that nobody uses. See, I'll have a
curtain stretched across the middle. You Chinese
set to work on this side. You Greeks work on the
other side. I'll give you a week. What about it?'

The artists agreed and set to work.

Every day the Chinese bowed low before the Sultan
with a list of colours. The Sultan threw open his
treasury. The Chinese assembled over a hundred

colours and were cheerfully busy behind the curtain all week.

And the Greeks?

They went to the Steward and asked for cleaning materials: rags, water, pumice-stone.

They, too, were happily busy throughout the week.

On the last day the Sultan came to inspect. The Chinese welcomed him with much banging of drums and tinkling of cymbals. When the Sultan entered their side he reeled back in astonishment. Dazzling splendour, glowing designs, multi-coloured patterns and artistry met his eyes.

Then he moved to the Greeks' side – but they stopped him and simply pulled back the curtain.

They had spent the week polishing the walls until every mark was removed. The walls shone – a perfect mirror, reflecting back, with even greater splendour, the work of the Chinese.

Tell You Later!

*H*E WAS HAPPILY asleep in the pleasant shade of a tree when, suddenly, he got a painful awakening. A man had dismounted from his horse and was raining down blow after blow on him with a stick.

'What's this? Stop! Help!' he yelled, but the blows continued. Up he jumped and ran off into the orchard. But his assailant followed, still striking him. He collapsed in agony beneath an apple tree.

'Now!' cried the attacker, throwing down his stick, 'start eating.' He picked up a squelchy rotten apple.

'No, no! What the – ' but the man pushed the apple into his mouth and forced it down.

'Now have another – '

'Ugghhh!'

'And another!'

'I can't, I can't –'

'Force it down! That's it. Now another . . .'

Apple followed apple. The victim struggled and spluttered. As soon as he opened his mouth another rotten apple went in.

'Help!' – a further apple – 'Mercy!' – another one – 'What have I done' – there was no let-up – 'to deserve this? Ugghh! Help, help! I can't take another one, I'm full –'

'Just one more. Now!' The stick was taken up again and a further beating rained down. Off the poor man ran but his attacker followed, his ears deaf to all screams for mercy. Down he fell and was beaten till he got to his feet. On he ran, on and on, all the while the rotten apples churning up inside.

At last he collapsed in sheer agony and was violently sick – and out of his mouth shot an evil-looking black snake. He gaped at it in astonishment, then up at his tormentor.

'You saved my life!' he cried.

The man smiled. 'I was passing and I saw it go down while you were asleep', he said. 'If I had

woken you and merely told you what had
happened, you would probably have died of terror
on the spot!'

The Two Slaves

*A*S THEY WERE being offered at bargain prices, the King bought two slaves and handed them over to his vizier to see what sort of work they were fit for. In due course he decided to have a word with them to find out how they were getting on. He sent for the first one.

He was pleased with what he saw. 'He would be all the better for a good scrub, of course,' he said to himself, 'and that can be put right.' But when he conversed with the lad he was quite delighted. He found that he had his wits about him, was pleasantly spoken and friendly – a real bargain in fact.

The second slave was sent for.

The King was no so well-pleased with this one. His teeth were black and crooked and, when he came near, his breath was not too pleasant, either.

'Er, yes, well,' said the King, 'if you wouldn't mind

standing further off? Yes, that will do. I will speak with you shortly.'

He turned to the first slave.

'Now, my lad,' he said with a smile, 'off to the bath-house with you. Tell them to give you a good scrub and a clean robe, and then you should be quite presentable.'

When the slave had gone, the King turned to the second slave.

'Well, now,' he said, 'I hear great things of you. Apparently you have the makings of an excellent secretary – or so I am told. I have sent for you so that we can talk together and I can then get an idea of how your mind works. You have – er – some superficial faults, but these can soon be attended to, I hope. No, it's what goes on *inside* that really matters to me. Now, from what my vizier tells me, you are worth a hundred slaves, not one! Yet, it puzzles me that your fellow-slave – the one I've just sent for a bath – should be so critical of you. Yes, if I believed him I would have to be disgusted with you. He says you are a thief, generally dishonest, even immoral, and that your reputation is well-known. Now, what have you to say to that?'

'He is usually a truthful fellow, my Lord,' the slave replied. 'Indeed, now I come to think of it, I doubt if I have ever come across one so truthful. And he is not malicious. The only thing I can think is that he sees faults in me that I can't see myself. Yes, that must be it.'

'Well, well,' said the King. 'But now, tell me this: does *he* have any faults, then, that only *you* can see? I want you to be as frank as he is. That's a quality I look for in all my servants, you know.'

'I will tell you his faults, if you wish, O King, though I must say I have always enjoyed working with him. His faults are that he is friendly, quick-witted, always good company. His biggest fault is his generosity. I believe he would readily give even his life if called upon to do so.'

'I see . . .'

'Another fault is his complete lack of self-conceit. He always blames himself if anything goes wrong. He's always unfailingly kind to others, and also –'

'Come, come,' interrupted the King, 'don't fall over yourself to heap praises upon him. I want you to be honest and indeed I hope you have been truthful.

I intend to put him to the test, so if you have been
lying you will be embarrassed, to say the least.'

However, the slave persisted in his good opinion.

When the first slave returned from the bath, the
King greeted him. 'Well well, what an
improvement! You're a handsome fellow, no doubt
about it. Alas, if it weren't for what I've just been
told by your fellow slave here, the sight of your face
would gladden my heart.'

'Why, O King?' asked the slave. 'What has the
fellow been saying about me?'

'Oh, many things,' said the King. 'I can't repeat
them all, but he tells me that you are two-faced, for
one thing, and for another that, though you appear
to be a cure for all ills, you are in fact the cause of
them.'

The slave was furious. He reddened with anger and
uncontrollably burst out: 'I knew it! I knew it! From
the moment I met that dog I knew that he was a
liar and scandalmonger! The foul-mouthed
creature, the dirty-minded – '

But the King put his hand over the gabbling slave's
mouth.

'Peace', he said. 'Enough, enough. It was but a trial to distinguish the merits of the two of you. Now I see that though you are good-looking, your spirit is ugly, whereas your companion is so only in his breath. You're the one I must now ask to sit far from me, and he it is I must bring near to me in the running of my affairs.'

As Far as the Ant Can See . . .

A TINY ANT saw a pen writing and scurried off until it met another ant.

'It was wonderful!' it cried. 'You should have seen the pen making pictures and patterns, like flowers in a garden.'

'Ah,' said the second ant, 'it isn't the *pen* that is the artist, actually, but the *finger*. In your excitement I don't suppose you noticed that. The pen is merely the instrument.'

'Excuse me,' said a third ant, 'but I couldn't help over-hearing, and I hope you don't mind my interrupting to tell you that, in fact, the fingers would be useless without the *arm*. That finger you mentioned would be helpless without it.'

'You're all wrong,' said a fourth ant. 'You see . . .' but you can imagine the discussion that went on. Eventually, the argument reached the ears of the chief of the ants, an old and wise being who

remarked: 'Beyond all this talk of physical things –
pen, finger, arm and so on – are the mind and spirit
of the Artist himself. What you speak of is but the
garment on the body.'

And these were but ants!

O you, who now read what the pen was writing,
how much further can *you* see?

True Love

*A*T LAST, after many setbacks and disappointments, a man found himself face to face with the one he had adored from afar. What did he do? He produced a letter and read to her! The letter was really a long poem, full of praise, sorrow at being parted from her, cries of pain – and all in exquisite verse.

She soon got tired.

'What a waste of time!' she cried. 'Here am I, beside you, and you read a letter! Are we lovers or not?'

'You don't understand!' he sighed. 'I want to experience every aspect of you: the radiance of the fountain, as well as the cool drink, the –'

'Oh stop!' cried the girl. 'You're just in love with being in love, not with me! On you go, rhapsodising about money in the bank while here I wait, cash in hand!'

The Marvellous Turban

A HOLY MAN made himself a magnificent turban. It was larger than anyone else's, and richly decorated with expensive silks. However, inside it was stuffed with bits of old rag, rotten cotton and mouldy bits of fur. No-one but himself knew this as, each day he paraded himself in the city and places of learning.

Early one morning, when he was on his way to the college, wearing this masterpiece, a thief pounced, knocked him down and ran off with it.

The holy man shouted after him.

'Thief, you can have my turban if you really want it. But I do beg you to examine it first. Feel inside. Then, if you still want it, you're welcome.'

The thief stopped and pulled the turban open. Out fell all the rotten rags.

'You old fraud!' cried the thief. 'You're doing me out of business!'

'We're both frauds, then,' sighed the holy man. 'But, see, the truth has taught us both a lesson!'

Layla and the Caliph

'SO YOU ARE Layla!' said the Caliph. 'You're the beauty that has sent my friend Majnun out of his mind with love for you. I can't understand it. To me you are no more beautiful than other women.'

'But you are not Majnun, my Lord,' Layla replied.

The Ride-a-Cock-
Horse Saint

*...and other tales
of the wisdom of the humble*

The Ride-a-Cock-Horse Saint

'*I*'VE GOT A problem,' said a visitor to the city. 'Are there any wise men here with whom I can discuss it?'

'The wisest among us,' said one of his hearers, 'is that fellow, there.' He pointed into the street, where an old man, astride a pole that he rode as a cock-horse, was playing among a crowd of noisy children.

'What, that man? You're having me on!'

'Try him and see.'

So the man with the problem approached the old man among the children.

'Old man, can you help me with a difficult problem?'

'Away with you!' cried the old man, galloping off across the street. 'Don't knock at my door,' he called over his shoulder, 'it's locked.'

'Come back, come back,' called the man. 'Ride my
way, just for a moment, I beg you.'

'Oh, all right,' said the old man, galloping over.
'What do you want, then? Be quick about it. My
horse is restive, as you can see. He's got quite a
temper, and if you're long winded he might kick you.'

Confronted by this child-like man on his stick, and
surrounded by the jeering children, the man
thought: How can I discuss the problems of my
heart in a situation like this? I suppose I might as
well play him along for a bit.

'I've decided to marry,' he said. 'Suppose I were to
choose a woman who lived on this street, for
example, who would you suggest would be the most
suitable for a man like me?'

'In this street, as in the world,' the old man replied,
'there are three kinds of woman: two of these will
bring sorrow to your soul. If you marry the first,
she will be wholly yours. Marry the second and she
will be only half yours. Marry the third and she
won't be yours at all. So now be off! And look out,
or my horse will kick out at you.'

And the old man rejoined the children.

'You must explain!' called the man. 'You can't just leave it like that.'

The old man rode back. 'Well, then,' he cried, 'if I must, I suppose I must. Marry a virgin and she will be wholly yours and a delight for ever. The one who is half yours is the childless widow. The one who will never be yours, even if you marry her, is the widow with a child, for her heart and her love are always with her child and her dead husband. So now – '

'Stay!' said the man, 'just one more question.'

'Be quick, be quick, then, for I long to be back among the children.'

'How is it that a man of your wisdom and obvious intelligence is playing a game like this?'

The old man sighed, dismounted, came over and whispered: 'It's like this. These fools are proposing to make me ruler of their city. It's the sort of job that would drive me mad. I protested, but they wouldn't have it. No, no, they said, By decree we are ordered to appoint the most superior one among us to recite the law – and you are the man. Hence this disguise, my friend. I pretend to be mad in order to keep my sanity.'

The Divine Mirror

'*M*Y, BUT HE'S an ugly fellow', said a Turk, little thinking that Mahommed would overhear.

'You're quite right', said Mohammed, 'impertinent, but undoubtedly right!'

Not long after this, an Indian, catching sight of Mohammed, exclaimed: 'O Sun of the World, shine on in beauty.'

'Friend', said Mahommed, 'you see beyond this world, and you see truly.'

Those who were with Mahommed said: 'O King, you commended both these men for telling the truth. Surely they can't both be right?'

'I'm just a mirror', Mahommed replied, 'polished by the hand of God. The two men, therefore, saw their own images, reflections of what is in themselves.'

Three Steps Up

*W*HEN UTHMAN BECAME Caliph, the moment arrived when he was about to mount the pulpit to preach. Now it was from this same pulpit that the Prophet Mohammed had once preached, and the pulpit was therefore regarded with reverence.

Uthman's predecessors had certainly done so.

Umar, for example, had never mounted higher than the first step, such was his awe and humility.

Abu Bakr had gone higher, but never beyond the second step.

Both Caliphs had been highly regarded by the people, who now watched to see what Uthman would do.

He mounted to the first step, then the second, then the third, and finally seated himself on the Throne itself!

This astonished all but it was received with respectful silence – apart from one man, well-known for his indiscreet chatter.

'How comes it', said he, 'that Uthman places himself up there on the Prophet's Throne? Umat and Abu Bakr never ventured to that height and they were certainly superior to him in rank.'

'This is how I see it', called Uthman. 'I thought to myself: If I stay on the first step, some of them will say: He is likening himself to Umar. If I stay on the second step, others will say: He is likening himself to Abu Bakr. But if I go the Prophet's place I shall be safe, since no-one can possibly imagine that I am likening myself to him!'

Ayaz and the Pearl Beyond Price

...and other tales of hypocrisy revealed

Ayaz and the Pearl Beyond Price

ONE DAY WHEN the King had all his courtiers round him he brought out a pearl that shone with such beauty that all gasped in admiration.

The King placed the pearl in the hands of his vizier. 'How much do you think it is worth?' he asked.

'More gold than could be carried by a hundred asses', the vizier replied.

'Smash it', ordered the King.

'My Lord!'

'Break it in pieces', the King insisted.

'But how can I possibly do that?' the vizier protested. 'I am in charge of your treasury. How could I, then, destroy a pearl of this value?'

'Well said!' the King proclaimed, and rewarded his vizier with several robes of honour. He took back the pearl and, for a while, the conversation turned to other matters.

Then suddenly the King placed the pearl in the hands of his chamberlain. 'How much do you think that would fetch on the market?' he asked.

'Your Majesty!' said the awed official, handling the pearl with care, 'this is worth half a kingdom.'

'Break it,' the King ordered.

'How can I do that?' begged the chamberlain. 'Regardless of its worth, look how beautiful it is, how it gleams. It shines brighter than the light of day. Who could destroy such beauty?'

'Well done,' said the King. 'You're an intelligent man as well as an appreciator of beauty.' He took back the pearl, gave the chamberlain a magnificent robe of honour and raised his salary on the spot.

In the course of the day, the King tried this on all the fifty or so courtiers. Each was ordered to destroy the pearl. Each refused and was rewarded.

Finally, the pearl was placed in the hands of Ayaz. 'Tell me, Ayaz, what value do you put on this pearl?'

'It is worth far more than I can say,' Ayaz replied.

'Break it into small fragments', the King ordered.

Ayaz placed the pearl on the ground, picked up a stone and in a few seconds had reduced the pearl to dust.

There was an outcry. When it had died down, Ayaz said:

'O, you great ones, which, then is more valuable: the command of my King, which you all broke, or this bit of coloured stone which I destroyed?'

A Greasy Tale

*H*E WAS A poor man and the courtiers usually ignored him. But this made him boast even more.

'Look at my moustache, is it greasy?' he would cry. 'Well, it's no wonder after the food I ate last night at a party! Such richness, such fatness. Mmmmm! Just look at my lips, friends, see how greasy they are, too. That comes of dining well, eh?'

'What a liar he is!' his poor belly rumbled. 'How I wish that greasy moustache were cut off! Down here I'm empty and in agony – and all because of his boasting. If he stopped telling everyone how well he'd dined, perhaps some courtier would take pity and fill me up!'

Well, the belly's wish was granted one day, through the boastful man's son. With a pale face, the obviously frightened little fellow pushed through the crowd, crying:

'My father, my father, the cat's run off with it!'

'With what, child?'

'Don't shout at me, don't beat me! I tried to stop the cat but it was too quick. And now, O now it's gone!'

'*What* has, fool?'

'That sheep's tail – the one you use every morning to grease your lips and moustache.'

Everyone had a good laugh at the red-faced man.

But then they also took pity on him – and began to invite him out to dinner. Down below, the belly gurgled happily while its owner, dining regularly on honest generosity, became honest himself and stopped his boasting.

The Townsman and the Countryman

THERE WAS ONCE a townsman who
became very friendly with a man from the
country. Whenever the countryman came to town
he stayed at the townsman's house as his guest.

'My house is yours', said the townsman. Meals,
lodging and every comfort were freely provided.

'You must let me repay this hospitality', the
countryman insisted. 'Now, when will you visit me
in the country? Come for a holiday. You should see
the countryside in the spring – Oh, the splendour of
the roses. Or, if you prefer, come in the summer,
when the fruit is ripe. Bring your whole family, your
relations, your servants. Now, when is it to be?'

But the townsman always put him off with some
excuse or other. 'We are expecting guests we haven't
seen for some years. Next year, perhaps, if I can get
away from my business.'

This went on year after year. At the end of his now

regular three month stay in town, the countryman would beg: 'My family are longing to meet you and your family. How long are you going to keep on promising? I feel ashamed to accept this lavish hospitality.'

'I'd love to come,' said the townsman, 'but it seems more and more impossible to get away. Next year, perhaps . . .'

Then the townsman's wife and children joined the pleas.

'Even the moon travels through the night sky, yet we always remain here in this spot. How nice it would be to have a holiday. Every year you lay more and more obligations on your friend – you must give him a chance to repay. He keeps begging us as well. Make him bring you to the country, he says. Do your best, coax him for my sake!'

So, beset on the one hand by the countryman's promises and on the other by his wife and children, the townsman at last gave in, and announced that they would have their holiday in the country.

What rejoicing followed! The whole house rang with cries of anticipation and the bustle of preparation.

'What fun we'll have!'

'Fresh fruit!'

'The open fields!'

'Shady orchards!'

'O the joys of travel!' the family cried. 'Like the moon, how full we shall grow with the experiences of our journey.' So, chattering and singing, riding and dancing, they continued their journey.

In fact, it took them longer than they anticipated. The village they thought was the countryman's had never heard of him. Nothing daunted, they tried the next, and the next – and nearly a whole month went by until, at last, they arrived at the correct one.

They were by now in a sorry state. They had had to sell the animals to buy food. Their shoes were worn out, their clothes were in rags. How relieved they were that the villagers recognised the name of the countryman. Quickly they sped to the house.

But no sooner had they arrived than the doors slammed shut and the sound of bolts being drawn was heard. They banged at the doors, and cried out

for hours, but there was no response from inside.
For five days they remained there, shivering with
cold by night, burning in the sun by day.

At length the countryman came out.

'Friend!' cried the townsman, 'don't you recognise
me? I'm the man at whose house you have stayed
all these many years. Here we all are, at last, at your
invitation!'

'What nonsense is this?' the countryman said.
'How can I recognise whoever you are in all that
filth? You could be a beggar or a king, for all I know.
I've never heard of you, or seen you before. Be off
with you!'

'But all these years, for months on end –'

'What absolute rubbish!' snapped the countryman,
withdrawing rapidly into his house and slamming
the door.

That night the sky emptied itself of rain in a
thunderstorm, drenching the impoverished family.
In absolute distress, the townsman battered on the
door until at last the servants had to get the
countryman from his bed.

'What is it now?' he demanded. 'I thought I told you –'

'Please,' begged the townsman, 'forget all I said, I make no claims on you. We've suffered five days now at your door – it seems like five years. All we ask for is a shed, a nook, a cranny – somewhere we can all creep into out of this terrible storm. Anywhere will do!'

'Well,' said the countryman, 'there *is* an old shed at the other end of the vineyard. It's the place for the vineyard keeper who has just left me. You can go there – but if you do you'll have to take his job on. You'll find bows and arrows somewhere. The job is to keep off the wolves. If you take it on, well, you're welcome to the shed. If not, you'd better move on.'

'I'll take it!' cried the desperate townsman. 'At the other end of the vineyard, did you say . . . ?'

So the shivering family crowded into the shed. There was hardly room to move. Everyone was crying, wishing with all their hearts that they had never left their comfortable town house.

Yet this was better than nothing and, afraid that they would be turned out of even the miserable shack if he did not guard the vineyard properly, the townsman took up the bows and arrows and stood on guard.

Suddenly he saw a shape approaching. It was animal of some kind. Trembling, he aimed an arrow and shot. There was cry – not from a wolf, but a donkey!

The donkey's cries brought out the enraged countryman.

'You idiot!' he shouted, 'you've shot one of my own beasts.'

'But I thought it was a wolf!' cried the townsman. 'It was my own donkey.'

'How can you be so sure in this darkness?' asked the townsman. 'Let's go and find out.'

'I don't need to,' said the countryman. 'I'd recognise the cry of that donkey even if it were three times as dark as this.'

'I knew it!' cried the townsman, losing all patience and springing on the countryman in fury. 'You recognised the cry of your donkey at midnight, you hypocrite. How then could you fail to know the voice of your host for these last ten years?'

A Servant of God

'*C* AUGHT YOU AT last!' cried the owner of the orchard, looking up into one of his trees. There, snaffling the dates, was the thief he had been seeking for a long time. 'Now you'll get what's coming to you!'

'Don't dare touch me', cried the thief. 'I'm a God-fearing man, and I belong to a group which believes that everything belongs to Him – '

'Oh yes?' said the owner, picking up a cudgel.

'Yes', said the thief. 'These dates are God's, my stomach is God's, and I am merely the servant of God, destined to bring the two together.' With this he gulped down another mouthful.

'Rascal!' roared the owner, 'I'll show you!' He reached up, grabbed the thief's ankles and pulled him down, tied him to the tree and began to beat him.

'Mercy!' shouted the thief.

'Now, I hope I've got it right', laughed the owner.
'This stick – *thwack!* – is God's, and your backside –
thwack! thwack! is God's. As for me, I am merely the
servant of God, destined – *thwack! thwack!* – to
bring the two together.'

'Mercy, mercy! I made it all up!'

'Pity! I was thinking of becoming a convert!' roared
the owner, still carrying on with the punishment.

Meat for the Cat

*...final tales of guests
and their experiences*

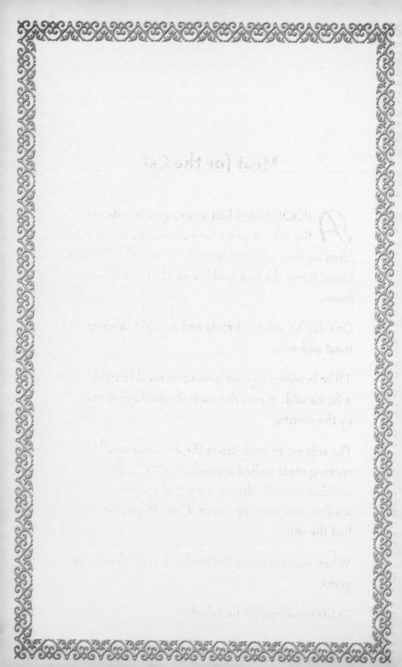

Meat for the Cat

Meat for the Cat

A POOR MAN had a very greedy wife. For the sake of peace he put up with it, but quite often he went without his meal because by the time he got home she had gobbled up all the food in the house.

One day he went out early and brought in some meat and wine.

'I'll be bringing a guest home to a meal tonight, wife,' he said. 'Here's the meat. Please have it ready by the evening.'

The wife set to work. Soon the delicious smell of cooking meat wafted through the house. She couldn't resist it. She ate a piece of meat, then another, and another - soon it had all gone. And so had the wine.

When evening came the husband arrived with the guest.

'Is the meal ready?' he asked.

'You'll have to go out and buy some more meat!' cried the wife.

'Buy more meat? What happened to the meat I brought in this morning?'

'The cat ate it all.'

'I don't believe it!'

'It's true.'

The husband grabbed hold of the cat and dumped it on the household scales.

'Four kilos, wife!' he shouted. 'Now I know the cat weighs four kilos and I know I bought four kilos of meat. So if this is the cat, where is the meat? Or, if this is the meat, where's the cat?'

The Sufi and His Donkey

A TRAVELLING SUFI arrived at a monastery one evening and was invited to stay the night. He took his donkey to the stable, left him with the servant there, and went in to join the monks. After a period of prayer, they sat down to a meal together.

Catching sight of the stable servant at the table, the Sufi remarked that he trusted that the animal was all right.

'Have no fear, sir,' the servant replied.

'I hope it has enough straw to rest on, and that the barley is of good quality?'

'God be gracious!' muttered the servant. 'What is he going on about? I've been doing this job for years. I should know how to stable a donkey by now!'

But the Sufi persisted.

'Do you mind if I suggest that you wet his barley

before giving it to him? He's an old donkey and his teeth are a bit shaky.'

'God be gracious, sir,' said the servant, barely concealing his irritation. 'Why are you telling me all this? I assure you I'm not without experience in these things.'

'And I'd be glad if you would take off his saddle and put some ointment on his back.'

'God be gracious, sir, you're not the first visitor we've had, you know! Thousands of guests have stayed here – and both they *and* their animals have gone away more than satisfied with their lodging, I can assure you.'

'As for his water, I wonder if you would mind warming it? Not much, just to take the sharpness out of it?'

'God be gracious, sir, you're beginning to embarrass me.'

'Oh, and another thing about the barley, if you don't mind? Don't put too much straw in it, will you?'

'God be gracious, spare me any further – '

'As for his stable, I know you'll see that it is swept

clear of stones and dung. But if it's wet, could you sprinkle dry earth on it?'

'God be –'

'And please don't forget to brush him. He likes that.'

' – Gracious! Reverend sir, have done! What's the point of all this? I do know my business!' With that the servant got up in anger and made off.

Now the servant, in spite of all his protestations, was an idle rascal. Off he went, not to the stable, but to join his friends for a night out.

Meanwhile, the Sufi, tired because of his journey, lay down to sleep. However, he was disturbed by bad dreams. They were all about his poor donkey.

First, he dreamed that the donkey had been attacked by a wolf which tore him to pieces. The Sufi woke up in great distress.

'Oh,' he sighed after a few moments, 'I'm sure he's all right. That servant seemed to know his business.'

Then he dreamed that his donkey was going along a road and that he fell, first into a ditch, and then down a well where he brayed in anguish.

'Oh, what shall I do?' cried the Sufi. 'If I knew where that servant slept ... I wonder if I should go out myself – but no, the doors will be locked and it will mean getting people up. I feel sure that servant was reliable – why, we shared our meal together, he and I. Yes, yes, I'm certain all is well.'

In fact, the animal was far from well. Restless and exhausted, in a filthy stable full of stones and dirt, his saddle crooked and his halter torn, he had no food of any kind. Barley with just a little straw? He'd have been grateful just for the straw!

At dawn the servant returned, jerked the saddle into position, kicked the donkey to his feet, and pushed it towards his waiting master.

The Sufi said farewell, and mounted, but the donkey had gone only a few steps when he fell to his knees.

'What's the matter with him?' the monks called out.

The Sufi dismounted and a brief inspection told him all too quickly how badly his animal had fared.

'Alas,' he said, indicating the servant, 'having spent the night in the God-be-gracious holiness of this fellow, there is no wonder that my donkey begins the day on his knees!'

A House called 'If'

$\mathcal{A}$ MAN ARRIVED from a far country and was anxious to find a house for himself and his family.

His friend pointed to a house in ruins.

'Look at that!' he said. 'If only it had a roof, that would be ideal. And if it had another room built on to it, why, I could come and stay with you!'

'A wonderful idea,' the man replied. 'If only it were possible to lodge in an 'If'!'

The Phantom Guest

IT WAS RATHER late in the afternoon when the guest arrived. Nevertheless he was welcomed with great joy by the master of the house – he was an old friend and there was much to talk about.

The wife, however, was not too pleased.

That night there was a festival in the area and she had been looking forward to it. Knowing this, her husband persuaded her that she must go, while he would stay at home with their guest.

Before she left, the wife said to her husband:

'Get the servants to put our bed near the door, and put our guest's bed in the corner where it is warmer.' Off she went to the festival.

The two friends had a happy time over the fruit and wine until well after midnight. Then the guest, tired after his journeying indicated that he would like to retire. He got up and went over to the bed by the door.

The master of the house was a little taken aback and refrained, from delicacy, from saying: That's not your bed – this is yours, over here.

In no time his guest had undressed and was fast asleep in the wrong bed.

That night it rained and rained. When in the early hours, the wife returned, she was soaked to the skin. Not wanting to disturb the household she did not light the lamp, but crept into the bed by the door. She snuggled up to the guest, gave him a kiss, and said:

'Husband, we're fated! The roads are now a quagmire. By morning it will be impossible for anyone to move about – and that means we're stuck with our dear guest for days, perhaps weeks! What a calamity! What a bore!'

Up rose the guest at once. 'That's quite enough!' he shouted. 'Where are my boots? Quagmire or not, I'm off. My curses upon both of you!'

The wife was stricken with shame.

'It was a joke!' she cried. 'Please don't go. Don't take offence. I was only having fun.'

But the guest had gone, leaving husband and wife to their shame and sorrow.

The phantom of their unwelcome guest haunted them for many a long year.